50 Delicious Vegan BBQ Recipes for Home

By: Kelly Johnson

Table of Contents

- Grilled Portobello Mushrooms
- BBQ Jackfruit Sandwiches
- Grilled Corn on the Cob
- Vegan BBQ Tofu Skewers
- BBQ Cauliflower Wings
- Grilled Vegetable Kebabs
- Vegan Pulled "Pork" Sandwiches
- Grilled Sweet Potatoes
- BBQ Tempeh Ribs
- Grilled Pineapple Slices
- BBQ Lentil Sliders
- Grilled Asparagus
- BBQ Chickpea Burgers
- Grilled Zucchini
- Vegan BBQ Pizza
- Grilled Eggplant Steaks
- BBQ Seitan Skewers
- Grilled Artichokes
- Vegan BBQ Meatballs
- Grilled Avocado
- BBQ Black Bean Burgers
- Grilled Peaches
- BBQ Mushroom Sliders
- Grilled Bell Peppers
- BBQ Soy Curls
- Grilled Tofu Steaks
- BBQ Chickpea Salad
- Grilled Tomato Bruschetta
- BBQ Cauliflower Steaks
- Grilled Watermelon
- BBQ Seitan Ribs
- Grilled Portobello Burgers
- BBQ Lentil Meatballs
- Grilled Baby Potatoes
- BBQ Tempeh Sandwiches

- Grilled Radicchio
- BBQ Chickpea Kebabs
- Grilled Stuffed Peppers
- BBQ Black Eyed Pea Burgers
- Grilled Brussels Sprouts
- BBQ Tofu Sandwiches
- Grilled Carrots
- BBQ Bean Salad
- Grilled Plantains
- BBQ Falafel
- Grilled Pineapple Salsa
- BBQ Spaghetti Squash
- Grilled Mango
- BBQ Beyond Burgers
- Grilled Polenta

Grilled Portobello Mushrooms

Ingredients:

- 4 large portobello mushrooms
- 1/4 cup balsamic vinegar
- 2 tablespoons olive oil
- 2 tablespoons soy sauce or tamari (for gluten-free)
- 2 cloves garlic, minced
- 1 teaspoon dried basil
- 1 teaspoon dried oregano
- Salt and pepper to taste

Instructions:

1. Prepare the Marinade:
    - In a bowl, whisk together the balsamic vinegar, olive oil, soy sauce, minced garlic, dried basil, and dried oregano.
    - Season the marinade with salt and pepper to taste.
2. Marinate the Mushrooms:
    - Clean the portobello mushrooms by gently wiping them with a damp paper towel.
    - Remove the stems and place the mushrooms gill-side up in a shallow dish.
    - Pour the marinade over the mushrooms, ensuring they are well coated.
    - Let them marinate for at least 30 minutes, flipping halfway through.
3. Preheat the Grill:
    - Preheat your grill to medium-high heat.
4. Grill the Mushrooms:
    - Place the marinated mushrooms on the grill, gill-side down.
    - Grill for about 5-7 minutes per side, or until the mushrooms are tender and have nice grill marks.
    - Brush with additional marinade during grilling if desired.
5. Serve:
    - Remove the mushrooms from the grill and let them rest for a few minutes.
    - Serve the grilled portobello mushrooms as a main dish, in burgers, or sliced over salads.

Enjoy your delicious and flavorful grilled portobello mushrooms!

BBQ Jackfruit Sandwiches

Ingredients:

- 2 cans young green jackfruit in water or brine, drained and rinsed
- 1 tablespoon olive oil
- 1 onion, finely chopped
- 3 cloves garlic, minced
- 1 cup BBQ sauce (make sure it's vegan)
- 1 tablespoon soy sauce or tamari (for gluten-free)
- 1 teaspoon smoked paprika
- 1/2 teaspoon chili powder
- 1/4 teaspoon black pepper
- 1/4 teaspoon salt
- Burger buns or sandwich rolls
- Optional toppings: coleslaw, pickles, avocado, lettuce

Instructions:

1. Prepare the Jackfruit:
    - Drain and rinse the canned jackfruit.
    - Use your hands or a fork to shred the jackfruit pieces into a "pulled" texture, discarding any seeds or tough core parts.
2. Cook the Onion and Garlic:
    - Heat the olive oil in a large skillet over medium heat.
    - Add the chopped onion and cook until softened, about 5 minutes.
    - Add the minced garlic and cook for another 1-2 minutes until fragrant.
3. Add the Jackfruit:
    - Add the shredded jackfruit to the skillet and stir to combine with the onion and garlic.
    - Cook for about 5 minutes, allowing the jackfruit to heat through and start to brown slightly.
4. Season the Jackfruit:
    - Add the BBQ sauce, soy sauce, smoked paprika, chili powder, black pepper, and salt to the skillet.
    - Stir well to coat the jackfruit evenly with the sauce and spices.
    - Reduce the heat to low and let the mixture simmer for about 15-20 minutes, stirring occasionally, until the jackfruit is tender and the flavors are well combined.
5. Assemble the Sandwiches:
    - Toast the burger buns or sandwich rolls if desired.
    - Spoon the BBQ jackfruit mixture onto the bottom half of each bun.
    - Add your desired toppings, such as coleslaw, pickles, avocado, or lettuce.
    - Place the top half of the bun on the sandwich.
6. Serve:

- Serve the BBQ jackfruit sandwiches immediately, with extra BBQ sauce on the side if desired.

Enjoy your flavorful and satisfying BBQ jackfruit sandwiches!

Grilled Corn on the Cob

Ingredients:

- 4 ears of corn, husked
- 2 tablespoons olive oil or melted vegan butter
- Salt to taste
- Pepper to taste
- Optional: lime wedges, chopped fresh herbs (such as cilantro or parsley), smoked paprika, vegan Parmesan

Instructions:

1. Prepare the Corn:
    - Husk the corn and remove all the silk.
    - Rinse the ears of corn under cold water.
2. Preheat the Grill:
    - Preheat your grill to medium-high heat.
3. Season the Corn:
    - Brush each ear of corn with olive oil or melted vegan butter.
    - Season with salt and pepper to taste.
4. Grill the Corn:
    - Place the corn directly on the grill grates.
    - Grill for about 10-15 minutes, turning every 2-3 minutes, until the corn is tender and has nice char marks all over.
5. Optional Garnishes:
    - Remove the corn from the grill and let it cool slightly.
    - Squeeze fresh lime juice over the corn.
    - Sprinkle with chopped fresh herbs, smoked paprika, or vegan Parmesan if desired.
6. Serve:
    - Serve the grilled corn on the cob hot as a side dish or snack.

Enjoy your perfectly grilled corn on the cob!

Vegan BBQ Tofu Skewers

Ingredients:

- 1 block extra-firm tofu, pressed and cubed
- 1 cup BBQ sauce (make sure it's vegan)
- 1 tablespoon soy sauce or tamari (for gluten-free)
- 1 tablespoon olive oil
- 1 teaspoon smoked paprika
- 1 teaspoon garlic powder
- 1 teaspoon onion powder
- 1 red bell pepper, cut into chunks
- 1 yellow bell pepper, cut into chunks
- 1 zucchini, sliced into thick rounds
- 1 red onion, cut into chunks
- Wooden or metal skewers

Instructions:

1. Press the Tofu:
    - Press the tofu to remove excess moisture. You can do this by wrapping the tofu block in paper towels and placing a heavy object on top for about 15-20 minutes.
2. Prepare the Marinade:
    - In a bowl, mix the BBQ sauce, soy sauce, olive oil, smoked paprika, garlic powder, and onion powder.
3. Marinate the Tofu:
    - Cut the pressed tofu into 1-inch cubes.
    - Place the tofu cubes in a shallow dish or a resealable plastic bag.
    - Pour half of the marinade over the tofu, reserving the other half for basting later.
    - Toss to coat the tofu evenly with the marinade.
    - Marinate in the refrigerator for at least 30 minutes, or up to 2 hours for more flavor.
4. Prepare the Vegetables:
    - Cut the bell peppers, zucchini, and red onion into chunks similar in size to the tofu cubes.
5. Assemble the Skewers:
    - If using wooden skewers, soak them in water for at least 30 minutes to prevent burning.
    - Thread the marinated tofu cubes and vegetable chunks onto the skewers, alternating between tofu and vegetables.
6. Preheat the Grill:
    - Preheat your grill to medium-high heat.
7. Grill the Skewers:
    - Place the skewers on the grill.

- Grill for about 10-15 minutes, turning every 2-3 minutes and basting with the reserved marinade, until the tofu is heated through and has nice grill marks, and the vegetables are tender.
8. Serve:
    - Remove the skewers from the grill and let them cool slightly.
    - Serve the BBQ tofu skewers hot, with additional BBQ sauce on the side if desired.

Enjoy your delicious and hearty vegan BBQ tofu skewers!

BBQ Cauliflower Wings

Ingredients:

- 1 large head of cauliflower, cut into bite-sized florets
- 1 cup all-purpose flour (or gluten-free flour blend)
- 1 cup unsweetened almond milk (or other plant-based milk)
- 1 teaspoon garlic powder
- 1 teaspoon onion powder
- 1 teaspoon smoked paprika
- 1/2 teaspoon salt
- 1/4 teaspoon black pepper
- 1 cup breadcrumbs (optional, for extra crunch)
- 1 cup BBQ sauce (make sure it's vegan)

Instructions:

1. Preheat the Oven:
    - Preheat your oven to 450°F (230°C).
    - Line a baking sheet with parchment paper or lightly grease it.
2. Prepare the Batter:
    - In a large bowl, whisk together the flour, almond milk, garlic powder, onion powder, smoked paprika, salt, and black pepper until smooth.
    - If using, place the breadcrumbs in a separate bowl.
3. Coat the Cauliflower:
    - Dip each cauliflower floret into the batter, letting any excess drip off.
    - If using breadcrumbs, roll the battered florets in the breadcrumbs to coat.
    - Place the coated florets on the prepared baking sheet in a single layer.
4. Bake the Cauliflower:
    - Bake in the preheated oven for 20-25 minutes, or until the coating is crisp and the cauliflower is tender.
5. Add the BBQ Sauce:
    - Remove the baked cauliflower from the oven.
    - Brush each floret generously with BBQ sauce.
    - Return to the oven and bake for an additional 10-15 minutes, or until the BBQ sauce is caramelized and sticky.
6. Serve:
    - Let the BBQ cauliflower wings cool slightly before serving.
    - Serve hot, with extra BBQ sauce or vegan ranch dressing for dipping if desired.

Enjoy your flavorful and satisfying BBQ cauliflower wings!

Grilled Vegetable Kebabs

Ingredients:

- 1 red bell pepper, cut into chunks
- 1 yellow bell pepper, cut into chunks
- 1 green bell pepper, cut into chunks
- 1 red onion, cut into chunks
- 1 zucchini, sliced into thick rounds
- 1 yellow squash, sliced into thick rounds
- 8-10 button mushrooms
- 1 cup cherry tomatoes
- 1/4 cup olive oil
- 2 tablespoons balsamic vinegar
- 2 cloves garlic, minced
- 1 teaspoon dried oregano
- 1 teaspoon dried basil
- 1 teaspoon smoked paprika
- Salt and pepper to taste
- Wooden or metal skewers

Instructions:

1. Prepare the Vegetables:
    - Wash and cut the vegetables into similar-sized chunks to ensure even cooking.
2. Make the Marinade:
    - In a small bowl, whisk together the olive oil, balsamic vinegar, minced garlic, dried oregano, dried basil, smoked paprika, salt, and pepper.
3. Marinate the Vegetables:
    - Place the cut vegetables in a large bowl or a resealable plastic bag.
    - Pour the marinade over the vegetables and toss to coat evenly.
    - Marinate for at least 30 minutes, or up to 2 hours for more flavor.
4. Prepare the Skewers:
    - If using wooden skewers, soak them in water for at least 30 minutes to prevent burning.
    - Thread the marinated vegetables onto the skewers, alternating colors and types of vegetables for a visually appealing mix.
5. Preheat the Grill:
    - Preheat your grill to medium-high heat.
6. Grill the Kebabs:
    - Place the vegetable skewers on the grill.
    - Grill for about 10-15 minutes, turning every few minutes to ensure even cooking, until the vegetables are tender and have nice grill marks.
7. Serve:
    - Remove the kebabs from the grill and let them cool slightly.

- Serve the grilled vegetable kebabs hot as a main dish or a side.

Enjoy your delicious and colorful grilled vegetable kebabs!

Vegan Pulled "Pork" Sandwiches

Ingredients:

- 2 cans young green jackfruit in water or brine, drained and rinsed
- 1 tablespoon olive oil
- 1 onion, finely chopped
- 3 cloves garlic, minced
- 1 cup BBQ sauce (make sure it's vegan)
- 1 tablespoon soy sauce or tamari (for gluten-free)
- 1 teaspoon smoked paprika
- 1/2 teaspoon chili powder
- 1/4 teaspoon black pepper
- 1/4 teaspoon salt
- 1/4 cup vegetable broth (optional, for juicier filling)
- Burger buns or sandwich rolls
- Optional toppings: coleslaw, pickles, avocado, lettuce

Instructions:

1. Prepare the Jackfruit:
    - Drain and rinse the canned jackfruit.
    - Use your hands or a fork to shred the jackfruit pieces into a "pulled" texture, discarding any seeds or tough core parts.
2. Cook the Onion and Garlic:
    - Heat the olive oil in a large skillet over medium heat.
    - Add the chopped onion and cook until softened, about 5 minutes.
    - Add the minced garlic and cook for another 1-2 minutes until fragrant.
3. Add the Jackfruit:
    - Add the shredded jackfruit to the skillet and stir to combine with the onion and garlic.
    - Cook for about 5 minutes, allowing the jackfruit to heat through and start to brown slightly.
4. Season the Jackfruit:
    - Add the BBQ sauce, soy sauce, smoked paprika, chili powder, black pepper, and salt to the skillet.
    - Stir well to coat the jackfruit evenly with the sauce and spices.
    - Add the vegetable broth if using, to make the filling juicier.
    - Reduce the heat to low and let the mixture simmer for about 15-20 minutes, stirring occasionally, until the jackfruit is tender and the flavors are well combined.
5. Assemble the Sandwiches:
    - Toast the burger buns or sandwich rolls if desired.
    - Spoon the BBQ jackfruit mixture onto the bottom half of each bun.
    - Add your desired toppings, such as coleslaw, pickles, avocado, or lettuce.
    - Place the top half of the bun on the sandwich.

6. Serve:
    - Serve the vegan pulled "pork" sandwiches immediately, with extra BBQ sauce on the side if desired.

Enjoy your delicious and hearty vegan pulled "pork" sandwiches!

Grilled Sweet Potatoes

Ingredients:

- 2 large sweet potatoes
- 2 tablespoons olive oil
- 1 teaspoon smoked paprika
- 1 teaspoon garlic powder
- 1 teaspoon onion powder
- 1/2 teaspoon salt
- 1/4 teaspoon black pepper
- Optional toppings: chopped fresh herbs (such as parsley or cilantro), vegan sour cream, lime wedges

Instructions:

1. Prepare the Sweet Potatoes:
    - Wash and peel the sweet potatoes.
    - Slice them into 1/4-inch thick rounds or wedges, ensuring they are evenly sized for uniform grilling.
2. Preheat the Grill:
    - Preheat your grill to medium-high heat.
3. Season the Sweet Potatoes:
    - In a large bowl, toss the sweet potato slices with olive oil to coat.
    - In a small bowl, mix together the smoked paprika, garlic powder, onion powder, salt, and black pepper.
    - Sprinkle the seasoning mixture over the sweet potatoes and toss to coat evenly.
4. Grill the Sweet Potatoes:
    - Place the sweet potato slices directly on the grill grates.
    - Grill for about 3-5 minutes per side, or until the sweet potatoes are tender and have nice grill marks. Keep an eye on them to prevent burning, and adjust the grill heat if necessary.
5. Serve:
    - Remove the grilled sweet potatoes from the grill and let them cool slightly.
    - Transfer to a serving platter and garnish with optional toppings like chopped fresh herbs, vegan sour cream, or a squeeze of lime juice.

Enjoy your delicious and nutritious grilled sweet potatoes!

BBQ Tempeh Ribs

Ingredients:

- 2 blocks tempeh
- 1/2 cup vegetable broth
- 1/4 cup soy sauce or tamari (for gluten-free)
- 1 tablespoon olive oil
- 1 tablespoon maple syrup
- 1 tablespoon apple cider vinegar
- 1 teaspoon smoked paprika
- 1 teaspoon garlic powder
- 1 teaspoon onion powder
- 1/2 teaspoon black pepper
- 1 cup BBQ sauce (make sure it's vegan)

Instructions:

1. Prepare the Tempeh:
    - Cut each block of tempeh in half lengthwise, then cut each piece into rib-sized strips.
2. Steam the Tempeh:
    - Place the tempeh strips in a steamer basket over boiling water.
    - Cover and steam for about 10 minutes. This helps to soften the tempeh and remove any bitterness.
3. Make the Marinade:
    - In a large bowl, whisk together the vegetable broth, soy sauce, olive oil, maple syrup, apple cider vinegar, smoked paprika, garlic powder, onion powder, and black pepper.
4. Marinate the Tempeh:
    - Place the steamed tempeh strips in a shallow dish or a resealable plastic bag.
    - Pour the marinade over the tempeh, ensuring all pieces are well coated.
    - Marinate in the refrigerator for at least 1 hour, or up to overnight for more flavor.
5. Preheat the Grill:
    - Preheat your grill to medium-high heat.
6. Grill the Tempeh Ribs:
    - Remove the tempeh from the marinade and brush with a layer of BBQ sauce.
    - Place the tempeh ribs on the grill.
    - Grill for about 3-5 minutes per side, brushing with additional BBQ sauce as they cook, until the tempeh is heated through and has nice grill marks.
7. Serve:
    - Remove the BBQ tempeh ribs from the grill.
    - Serve hot with extra BBQ sauce on the side if desired.

Enjoy your savory and satisfying BBQ tempeh ribs!

Grilled Pineapple Slices

Ingredients:

- 1 pineapple, peeled, cored, and cut into thick slices
- 2 tablespoons maple syrup or agave nectar
- 1 tablespoon lime juice
- 1 teaspoon ground cinnamon
- Optional: vanilla ice cream or coconut whipped cream for serving

Instructions:

1. Prepare the Pineapple:
    - Peel the pineapple and cut it into thick slices, about 1/2 to 3/4 inch thick.
    - Make sure to core each slice if not using pre-cored pineapple.
2. Make the Marinade:
    - In a small bowl, whisk together the maple syrup (or agave nectar), lime juice, and ground cinnamon.
3. Marinate the Pineapple:
    - Place the pineapple slices in a shallow dish or a resealable plastic bag.
    - Pour the marinade over the pineapple slices, turning them to coat evenly.
    - Let the pineapple marinate for about 15-30 minutes at room temperature, or longer in the refrigerator for a more intense flavor.
4. Preheat the Grill:
    - Preheat your grill to medium-high heat.
5. Grill the Pineapple:
    - Place the pineapple slices directly on the grill grates.
    - Grill for about 2-3 minutes per side, or until grill marks appear and the pineapple caramelizes slightly.
    - You can brush the slices with any remaining marinade while grilling for extra flavor.
6. Serve:
    - Remove the grilled pineapple slices from the grill and let them cool slightly.
    - Serve them warm as a dessert or a side dish.
    - Optionally, serve with a scoop of vanilla ice cream or a dollop of coconut whipped cream for a delightful treat.

Enjoy your delicious grilled pineapple slices!

BBQ Lentil Sliders

Ingredients:

For the lentil patties:

- 1 cup dry green or brown lentils
- 2 cups vegetable broth or water
- 1/2 onion, finely chopped
- 2 garlic cloves, minced
- 1 tablespoon olive oil
- 1/2 teaspoon smoked paprika
- 1/2 teaspoon cumin
- 1/2 teaspoon chili powder
- Salt and pepper, to taste
- 1/2 cup breadcrumbs (gluten-free if needed)
- 1/4 cup barbecue sauce (plus extra for serving)

For assembling the sliders:

- Slider buns or small dinner rolls
- Barbecue sauce, for topping
- Coleslaw or lettuce, for serving (optional)
- Sliced pickles, for serving (optional)

Instructions:

1. Cook the lentils:
    - Rinse the lentils under cold water. In a saucepan, combine the lentils and vegetable broth (or water). Bring to a boil, then reduce the heat and simmer for about 20-25 minutes, or until the lentils are tender and most of the liquid is absorbed. Drain any excess liquid and set aside.
2. Prepare the lentil mixture:
    - In a large skillet, heat the olive oil over medium heat. Add the chopped onion and cook until softened, about 5 minutes. Add the minced garlic, smoked paprika, cumin, and chili powder. Cook for another 1-2 minutes until fragrant.
3. Make the lentil patties:
    - Transfer the cooked lentils to a large mixing bowl. Add the sautéed onion and garlic mixture, breadcrumbs, and barbecue sauce. Season with salt and pepper to taste. Mix until well combined.
    - Using your hands, shape the mixture into small patties, about 2-3 inches in diameter. Place the patties on a plate or baking sheet lined with parchment paper.
4. Cook the lentil patties:

- Heat a non-stick skillet or grill pan over medium-high heat. Cook the lentil patties for about 3-4 minutes on each side, or until golden brown and heated through. Brush each patty with additional barbecue sauce while cooking if desired.
5. Assemble the sliders:
    - Toast the slider buns or dinner rolls lightly if preferred. Place a lentil patty on the bottom half of each bun. Top with a dollop of barbecue sauce, coleslaw or lettuce, and sliced pickles if using. Cover with the top half of the bun.
6. Serve:
    - Arrange the BBQ Lentil Sliders on a serving platter and serve immediately. Enjoy these flavorful sliders as a main dish or appetizer!

Tips:

- Texture: Ensure the lentil mixture is well combined and holds together before shaping into patties. If it's too dry, add a bit more barbecue sauce or a splash of vegetable broth.
- Make ahead: You can prepare the lentil mixture and shape the patties ahead of time. Store them covered in the refrigerator until ready to cook.
- Variations: Customize your sliders with your favorite toppings such as sliced avocado, red onion, or a slice of cheese (if not vegan).

These BBQ Lentil Sliders are packed with protein and flavor, making them a satisfying vegetarian option for any occasion. They're sure to be a hit with both vegetarians and meat-lovers alike!

Grilled Asparagus

Ingredients:

- 1 bunch of asparagus spears
- 2 tablespoons olive oil
- Salt and pepper, to taste
- Optional: Lemon wedges, grated Parmesan cheese, balsamic glaze, or chopped herbs for serving

Instructions:

1. Prepare the asparagus:
   - Wash the asparagus spears under cold water and trim off the tough ends (usually about 1-2 inches from the bottom). You can snap off the ends where they naturally break or use a knife to trim them evenly.
2. Marinate (optional):
   - Place the trimmed asparagus spears in a shallow dish or zip-top bag. Drizzle with olive oil and season with salt and pepper. Toss gently to coat the asparagus evenly. You can also add a squeeze of lemon juice or minced garlic for extra flavor if desired. Let marinate for at least 15-30 minutes at room temperature.
3. Preheat the grill:
   - Preheat your grill to medium-high heat. If using a gas grill, close the lid and allow it to heat up for about 10 minutes. If using a charcoal grill, make sure the coals are hot and covered with ash before cooking.
4. Grill the asparagus:
   - Place the asparagus spears directly on the grill grate in a single layer. Arrange them perpendicular to the grill grates to prevent them from falling through.
   - Grill for about 3-5 minutes per side, or until the asparagus is tender and slightly charred, rotating them occasionally for even cooking. The cooking time will depend on the thickness of the asparagus spears.
5. Serve:
   - Remove the grilled asparagus from the grill and transfer to a serving platter. Drizzle with additional olive oil if desired and season with more salt and pepper to taste. Serve immediately while hot.
6. Optional toppings:
   - Garnish the grilled asparagus with lemon wedges for squeezing over the top, grated Parmesan cheese, a drizzle of balsamic glaze, or chopped fresh herbs like parsley or basil for added freshness and flavor.

Tips:

- Grill temperature: Ensure your grill is hot enough to create grill marks and a slight char without overcooking the asparagus. Medium-high heat is typically ideal.

- Asparagus thickness: Thicker asparagus spears will take slightly longer to grill, while thinner ones will cook more quickly. Adjust the cooking time accordingly.
- Alternative cooking methods: If you don't have a grill, you can also roast the asparagus in the oven at 400°F (200°C) for about 10-15 minutes, or until tender and lightly browned.

Grilled asparagus is a versatile side dish that pairs well with a variety of main courses, from grilled meats to seafood and vegetarian dishes. Enjoy its delicious flavors and crispy texture straight from the grill!

BBQ Chickpea Burgers

Ingredients:

For the chickpea patties:

- 2 cans (15 ounces each) chickpeas, drained and rinsed
- 1/2 cup breadcrumbs (gluten-free if needed)
- 1/4 cup barbecue sauce, plus extra for serving
- 1 tablespoon Dijon mustard
- 1 teaspoon smoked paprika
- 1/2 teaspoon garlic powder
- Salt and pepper, to taste
- 1 tablespoon olive oil (for cooking)

For assembling the burgers:

- Burger buns of your choice
- Lettuce leaves
- Sliced tomatoes
- Sliced red onion
- Sliced avocado (optional)
- Pickles (optional)

Instructions:

1. Prepare the chickpea mixture:
    - In a large mixing bowl, mash the chickpeas using a potato masher or fork until they are mostly mashed but still have some texture.
2. Add seasonings and binders:
    - Add the breadcrumbs, barbecue sauce, Dijon mustard, smoked paprika, garlic powder, salt, and pepper to the mashed chickpeas. Mix until well combined. Adjust seasoning to taste.
3. Form the patties:
    - Divide the chickpea mixture into 4 equal portions. Shape each portion into a patty using your hands. The mixture may be slightly sticky, so wetting your hands with water can help prevent sticking.
4. Cook the patties:
    - Heat olive oil in a large skillet over medium heat. Once hot, add the chickpea patties to the skillet. Cook for about 4-5 minutes on each side, or until golden brown and heated through. Brush each patty with additional barbecue sauce while cooking if desired.
5. Assemble the burgers:
    - Toast the burger buns lightly if preferred. Place a chickpea patty on the bottom half of each bun.

- Top with lettuce leaves, sliced tomatoes, sliced red onion, avocado slices (if using), and pickles. Drizzle extra barbecue sauce over the toppings if desired.
6. Serve:
    - Cover the burgers with the top half of the bun and serve immediately. Enjoy these flavorful BBQ Chickpea Burgers while hot!

Tips:

- Texture: Ensure the chickpea mixture is well combined and holds together before shaping into patties. If it's too dry, add a bit more barbecue sauce or a splash of water.
- Make ahead: You can prepare the chickpea mixture and shape the patties ahead of time. Store them covered in the refrigerator until ready to cook.
- Variations: Customize your burgers with your favorite toppings and condiments such as cheese, caramelized onions, or different types of sauces.

These BBQ Chickpea Burgers are packed with protein and flavor, making them a delicious vegetarian alternative to traditional burgers. They're sure to be a hit at your next barbecue or meal!

Grilled Zucchini

Ingredients:

- 2-3 medium zucchini
- 2 tablespoons olive oil
- 2 cloves garlic, minced (optional)
- 1 teaspoon dried Italian herbs (such as oregano, basil, thyme)
- Salt and pepper, to taste
- Fresh lemon juice (optional), for serving
- Fresh herbs (such as parsley or basil), chopped for garnish (optional)

Instructions:

1. Prepare the zucchini:
    - Wash the zucchini thoroughly and pat dry with paper towels. Trim off the ends and slice the zucchini into rounds, about 1/4 to 1/2 inch thick.
2. Marinate the zucchini (optional):
    - In a bowl, combine the olive oil, minced garlic (if using), dried Italian herbs, salt, and pepper. Toss the zucchini rounds in the marinade until evenly coated. Let them marinate for at least 15-30 minutes to absorb the flavors.
3. Preheat the grill:
    - Preheat your grill to medium-high heat. If using a gas grill, close the lid and allow it to heat up for about 10 minutes. If using a charcoal grill, make sure the coals are hot and covered with ash.
4. Grill the zucchini:
    - Place the zucchini rounds directly on the grill grates in a single layer. Grill for about 3-4 minutes per side, or until they are tender and have nice grill marks. Use a pair of tongs to flip them halfway through cooking.
5. Serve:
    - Remove the grilled zucchini from the grill and transfer to a serving platter. Squeeze fresh lemon juice over the zucchini if desired and sprinkle with chopped fresh herbs for garnish.
6. Enjoy:
    - Serve the grilled zucchini immediately while hot as a side dish or appetizer. It pairs well with grilled meats, seafood, or as part of a vegetarian meal.

Tips:

- Zucchini thickness: Keep the zucchini slices uniform in thickness to ensure even cooking.
- Grill temperature: Adjust the grill temperature as needed to prevent burning and ensure the zucchini cooks evenly.

- Variations: Experiment with different seasonings such as smoked paprika, lemon zest, or a sprinkle of Parmesan cheese after grilling.

Grilled zucchini is a healthy and versatile dish that highlights the natural flavors of this summer squash. It's quick to prepare and adds a delicious touch to any outdoor gathering or meal.

Vegan BBQ Pizza

Ingredients:

For the pizza dough (or use store-bought dough):

- 1 batch of pizza dough (homemade or store-bought)
- Flour, for dusting

For the BBQ sauce:

- 1/2 cup barbecue sauce (choose a vegan variety)
- 1 tablespoon tomato paste
- 1 tablespoon maple syrup or agave syrup
- 1 tablespoon soy sauce or tamari
- 1 clove garlic, minced
- 1/2 teaspoon smoked paprika
- Salt and pepper, to taste

For assembling the pizza:

- 1 cup shredded vegan mozzarella cheese (or other vegan cheese of choice)
- 1 cup sliced bell peppers (any color)
- 1/2 cup sliced red onion
- 1/2 cup sliced mushrooms
- Fresh cilantro or parsley, chopped (for garnish)
- Red pepper flakes (optional, for extra heat)

Instructions:

1. Preheat the oven:
   - Preheat your oven to the temperature specified for your pizza dough (usually around 450°F or 230°C). If you have a pizza stone, place it in the oven to preheat as well.
2. Prepare the BBQ sauce:
   - In a small bowl, mix together the barbecue sauce, tomato paste, maple syrup or agave syrup, soy sauce or tamari, minced garlic, smoked paprika, salt, and pepper. Adjust the sweetness and seasoning to your taste preferences. Set aside.
3. Prepare the toppings:
   - Prepare your vegetables by slicing the bell peppers, red onion, and mushrooms.
4. Roll out the pizza dough:
   - On a lightly floured surface, roll out the pizza dough to your desired thickness. Transfer the rolled-out dough onto a pizza peel or a lightly floured baking sheet.
5. Assemble the pizza:

- Spread a generous amount of the BBQ sauce mixture evenly over the rolled-out pizza dough, leaving a small border around the edges for the crust.
- Sprinkle the shredded vegan mozzarella cheese (or other vegan cheese of choice) evenly over the BBQ sauce.
- Arrange the sliced bell peppers, red onion, and mushrooms on top of the cheese.

6. Bake the pizza:
    - Carefully slide the assembled pizza onto the preheated pizza stone in the oven, or place the baking sheet directly in the oven.
    - Bake for about 12-15 minutes, or until the crust is golden brown and the cheese is melted and bubbly.
7. Finish and serve:
    - Remove the pizza from the oven and let it cool slightly. Sprinkle with chopped fresh cilantro or parsley and red pepper flakes (if using) for extra flavor and garnish.
    - Slice the Vegan BBQ Pizza and serve hot. Enjoy the delicious flavors of barbecue sauce and fresh vegetables!

Tips:

- Pizza dough: You can make your own pizza dough from scratch or use store-bought dough for convenience.
- Vegetable variations: Feel free to customize the toppings with your favorite vegetables such as cherry tomatoes, spinach, or grilled tofu for added protein.
- Grilling option: If you prefer, you can grill the pizza on a preheated grill instead of baking it in the oven. Cook the pizza over indirect heat with the grill lid closed until the crust is cooked and toppings are heated through.

This Vegan BBQ Pizza is perfect for pizza nights or any occasion where you want a tasty and satisfying plant-based meal. Enjoy creating and savoring this flavorful pizza recipe!

Grilled Eggplant Steaks

Ingredients:

- 2 large eggplants
- 1/4 cup olive oil
- 3 cloves garlic, minced
- 1 teaspoon dried oregano
- 1 teaspoon dried thyme
- Salt and pepper, to taste
- Fresh lemon juice, for serving
- Fresh herbs (such as parsley or basil), chopped for garnish (optional)

Instructions:

1. Prepare the eggplants:
    - Wash the eggplants and trim off the tops. Slice the eggplants lengthwise into 1/2-inch thick steaks. You can peel the eggplant or leave the skin on, depending on your preference.
2. Prepare the marinade:
    - In a small bowl, whisk together the olive oil, minced garlic, dried oregano, dried thyme, salt, and pepper.
3. Marinate the eggplant steaks:
    - Place the eggplant steaks in a shallow dish or a large zip-top bag. Pour the marinade over the eggplant steaks, ensuring they are evenly coated. Let them marinate for at least 15-30 minutes at room temperature, or up to 1-2 hours in the refrigerator for more flavor.
4. Preheat the grill:
    - Preheat your grill to medium-high heat. If using a gas grill, close the lid and allow it to heat up for about 10 minutes. If using a charcoal grill, make sure the coals are hot and covered with ash before cooking.
5. Grill the eggplant steaks:
    - Place the marinated eggplant steaks on the grill. Grill for about 3-4 minutes per side, or until the eggplant is tender and has distinct grill marks. Use a pair of tongs to flip the eggplant steaks carefully.
6. Serve:
    - Remove the grilled eggplant steaks from the grill and transfer to a serving platter. Squeeze fresh lemon juice over the eggplant steaks and sprinkle with chopped fresh herbs for garnish if desired.
7. Enjoy:
    - Serve the grilled eggplant steaks hot as a delicious vegetarian main course or side dish. They pair well with rice, quinoa, salads, or as part of a Mediterranean-inspired meal.

Tips:

- Eggplant selection: Choose firm and shiny eggplants with smooth skin for the best results.
- Grill temperature: Adjust the grill temperature as needed to prevent burning and ensure even cooking of the eggplant.
- Flavor variations: Customize the marinade with your favorite herbs and spices such as basil, rosemary, or smoked paprika for different flavor profiles.

Grilled eggplant steaks are a flavorful and nutritious dish that highlights the natural sweetness and texture of eggplant. They make a great addition to any summer barbecue or as a satisfying meal on their own. Enjoy grilling and savoring these delicious eggplant steaks!

BBQ Seitan Skewers

Ingredients:

- 1 pound seitan, cut into cubes or strips
- 1/2 cup barbecue sauce (choose a vegan variety)
- 2 tablespoons soy sauce or tamari
- 1 tablespoon maple syrup or agave syrup
- 1 tablespoon olive oil
- 1 clove garlic, minced
- 1/2 teaspoon smoked paprika
- Salt and pepper, to taste
- Bell peppers, cherry tomatoes, onions, or any other vegetables of choice, cut into chunks
- Wooden skewers, soaked in water for at least 30 minutes (to prevent burning)

Instructions:

1. Prepare the seitan marinade:
    - In a bowl, combine the barbecue sauce, soy sauce or tamari, maple syrup or agave syrup, olive oil, minced garlic, smoked paprika, salt, and pepper. Mix well to combine.
2. Marinate the seitan:
    - Place the seitan cubes or strips in a shallow dish or a large zip-top bag. Pour the marinade over the seitan, making sure each piece is coated evenly. Let it marinate for at least 30 minutes at room temperature, or refrigerate for up to 2 hours for more flavor.
3. Assemble the skewers:
    - Preheat your grill to medium-high heat. If using wooden skewers, soak them in water for at least 30 minutes to prevent burning.
    - Thread the marinated seitan cubes (and vegetables, if using) onto the skewers, alternating between seitan and vegetables to create colorful skewers.
4. Grill the skewers:
    - Lightly oil the grill grate. Place the seitan skewers on the grill, ensuring they are not overcrowded.
    - Grill for about 3-4 minutes per side, or until the seitan is heated through and has nice grill marks. Brush with any remaining marinade while grilling for extra flavor.
5. Serve:
    - Remove the BBQ Seitan Skewers from the grill and transfer to a serving platter. Serve hot, garnished with fresh herbs if desired.
6. Enjoy:
    - Serve the BBQ Seitan Skewers as a delicious main course or appetizer. They pair well with rice, quinoa, salads, or served with additional barbecue sauce for dipping.

Tips:

- Seitan options: You can use store-bought seitan or make your own at home. Adjust the cooking time based on the thickness of your seitan pieces.
- Vegetable variations: Customize the skewers with your favorite vegetables such as bell peppers, cherry tomatoes, onions, zucchini, or mushrooms.
- Grilling alternative: If you don't have a grill, you can cook these skewers in a grill pan on the stove or bake them in the oven at 400°F (200°C) for about 15-20 minutes, turning halfway through.

These BBQ Seitan Skewers are flavorful, satisfying, and perfect for outdoor grilling or any occasion where you want to enjoy a tasty vegan dish. Enjoy making and savoring these delicious skewers!

Grilled Artichokes

Ingredients:

- 2 large artichokes
- 1 lemon, halved
- 3 cloves garlic, minced
- 1/4 cup olive oil
- Salt and pepper, to taste
- Fresh herbs (such as parsley or thyme), chopped for garnish (optional)
- Lemon wedges, for serving

Instructions:

1. Prepare the artichokes:
   - Fill a large bowl with water and squeeze the juice of one lemon into it. This helps prevent the artichokes from turning brown.
   - Trim the artichokes: Start by removing the tough outer leaves until you reach the more tender inner leaves. Trim about 1/2 inch off the top of the artichoke and use a knife to trim the stem, leaving about 1 inch attached.
   - Cut the artichokes in half lengthwise and scoop out the choke (the fuzzy center) and any small inner leaves with a spoon.
   - Place each cleaned artichoke half into the lemon water to prevent them from browning while you prepare the grill.
2. Pre-cook the artichokes (optional):
   - If desired, you can pre-cook the artichokes in boiling water for about 10-15 minutes until slightly tender. This step helps reduce grilling time and ensures the artichokes are fully cooked through on the grill.
3. Prepare the marinade:
   - In a small bowl, whisk together the minced garlic, olive oil, salt, and pepper.
4. Grill the artichokes:
   - Preheat your grill to medium-high heat.
   - Remove the artichokes from the lemon water and pat them dry with paper towels.
   - Brush the cut sides of the artichokes generously with the garlic and olive oil mixture.
   - Place the artichokes cut-side down on the grill grates. Grill for about 5-7 minutes, or until they are charred and tender, rotating them halfway through cooking.
   - Flip the artichokes and grill for an additional 3-5 minutes, until they are heated through and nicely grilled on both sides.
5. Serve:
   - Remove the grilled artichokes from the grill and transfer them to a serving platter.
   - Squeeze fresh lemon juice over the artichokes and sprinkle with chopped fresh herbs (if using) for garnish.
   - Serve immediately while hot, with additional lemon wedges on the side.

Tips:

- Choosing artichokes: Look for firm and heavy artichokes with tightly packed leaves. Larger artichokes tend to have larger hearts, which are delicious when grilled.
- Grill temperature: Medium-high heat works best to achieve a nice char without burning the artichokes.
- Variations: You can add additional seasonings to the marinade, such as dried herbs like thyme or rosemary, or a sprinkle of grated Parmesan cheese after grilling for added flavor.

Grilled artichokes make a fantastic appetizer or side dish that pairs well with grilled meats, seafood, or as part of a vegetarian meal. Enjoy the delicious flavors and unique texture of grilled artichokes!

Vegan BBQ Meatballs

Ingredients:

For the meatballs:

- 1 can (15 ounces) chickpeas, drained and rinsed
- 1 cup cooked quinoa (or substitute with cooked lentils or brown rice)
- 1/2 cup breadcrumbs (gluten-free if needed)
- 1/4 cup finely chopped onion
- 2 cloves garlic, minced
- 2 tablespoons tomato paste
- 1 tablespoon soy sauce or tamari
- 1 tablespoon olive oil
- 1 teaspoon smoked paprika
- 1/2 teaspoon ground cumin
- Salt and pepper, to taste
- 1 tablespoon chopped fresh parsley or cilantro (optional)
- Oil for frying (such as olive oil or vegetable oil)

For the BBQ sauce:

- 1 cup barbecue sauce (choose a vegan variety)
- 2 tablespoons maple syrup or agave syrup
- 1 tablespoon apple cider vinegar
- 1 teaspoon Dijon mustard
- 1/2 teaspoon garlic powder
- Salt and pepper, to taste

Instructions:

1. Prepare the meatballs:
    - In a food processor, combine the chickpeas, cooked quinoa, breadcrumbs, onion, garlic, tomato paste, soy sauce or tamari, olive oil, smoked paprika, cumin, salt, and pepper. Pulse until well combined and the mixture holds together when pressed. You want a textured mixture, not completely smooth.
    - If the mixture is too dry, add a tablespoon of water or more tomato paste to help bind the ingredients together.
2. Form the meatballs:
    - Using your hands, roll the mixture into meatball-sized balls, about 1 to 1.5 inches in diameter. Place them on a plate or baking sheet lined with parchment paper.
3. Cook the meatballs:
    - Heat a large skillet over medium heat and add enough oil to coat the bottom of the skillet.
    - Once the oil is hot, add the meatballs in batches, making sure not to overcrowd the skillet. Cook for about 4-5 minutes, turning occasionally, until all sides are golden brown and crispy.

- Transfer the cooked meatballs to a plate lined with paper towels to absorb excess oil.
4. Make the BBQ sauce:
    - In a small saucepan, combine the barbecue sauce, maple syrup or agave syrup, apple cider vinegar, Dijon mustard, garlic powder, salt, and pepper. Stir well to combine.
    - Heat the sauce over medium-low heat, stirring occasionally, until warmed through and slightly thickened.
5. Combine meatballs with BBQ sauce:
    - Once all the meatballs are cooked and the sauce is ready, add the meatballs to the saucepan with the BBQ sauce.
    - Gently toss the meatballs in the sauce until they are well coated. Cook for an additional 2-3 minutes, stirring gently, to allow the flavors to meld together.
6. Serve:
    - Remove from heat and transfer the Vegan BBQ Meatballs to a serving dish. Sprinkle with chopped fresh parsley or cilantro if desired.
    - Serve the meatballs hot as a delicious appetizer or main dish. They pair well with rice, quinoa, or a fresh salad.

Tips:

- Texture: Ensure the chickpea mixture is well combined and holds together when forming into meatballs. Adjust the moisture content with additional tomato paste or water as needed.
- Baking option: If you prefer a healthier option, you can bake the meatballs in a preheated oven at 375°F (190°C) for about 20-25 minutes, turning halfway through, until golden brown and cooked through.
- Storage: Leftover meatballs can be stored in an airtight container in the refrigerator for up to 3-4 days. Reheat gently in the microwave or oven before serving.

These Vegan BBQ Meatballs are packed with flavor and protein, making them a satisfying and delicious option for vegans and non-vegans alike. Enjoy making and savoring these flavorful meatballs!

Grilled Avocado

Ingredients:

- 2 ripe avocados
- 1 tablespoon olive oil
- Salt and pepper, to taste
- Optional toppings: salsa, chopped tomatoes, cilantro, lime juice, or a sprinkle of smoked paprika

Instructions:

1. Prepare the avocados:
   - Cut the avocados in half lengthwise and remove the pits. Keep the skin on.
2. Preheat the grill:
   - Preheat your grill to medium-high heat.
3. Brush with olive oil:
   - Brush the cut sides of the avocados with olive oil. This helps prevent sticking and adds flavor.
4. Season:
   - Lightly sprinkle the cut sides of the avocados with salt and pepper, to taste.
5. Grill the avocados:
   - Place the avocados cut-side down on the grill grates. Grill for about 2-3 minutes, or until grill marks appear and the avocados are slightly warmed through.
6. Serve:
   - Carefully remove the grilled avocados from the grill and transfer them to a serving platter or individual plates.
   - Serve immediately while warm. Optionally, top with salsa, chopped tomatoes, cilantro, a squeeze of lime juice, or a sprinkle of smoked paprika for added flavor.

Tips:

- Avocado ripeness: Use ripe avocados that give slightly to gentle pressure. They should be firm but yield to a gentle squeeze.
- Grill temperature: Medium-high heat works best for grilling avocados to achieve nice grill marks without overcooking.
- Variations: Experiment with different toppings and seasonings to suit your taste preferences. Grilled avocado pairs well with a variety of flavors, so feel free to get creative!

Grilled avocado is a versatile dish that can be enjoyed as a side, appetizer, or part of a larger meal. It's quick to prepare and adds a delicious twist to your grilling repertoire. Enjoy the creamy texture and subtle smokiness of grilled avocados!

BBQ Black Bean Burgers

Ingredients:

- 2 ripe avocados
- 1 tablespoon olive oil
- Salt and pepper, to taste
- Optional toppings: salsa, chopped tomatoes, cilantro, lime juice, or a sprinkle of smoked paprika

Instructions:

1. Prepare the avocados:
    - Cut the avocados in half lengthwise and remove the pits. Keep the skin on.
2. Preheat the grill:
    - Preheat your grill to medium-high heat.
3. Brush with olive oil:
    - Brush the cut sides of the avocados with olive oil. This helps prevent sticking and adds flavor.
4. Season:
    - Lightly sprinkle the cut sides of the avocados with salt and pepper, to taste.
5. Grill the avocados:
    - Place the avocados cut-side down on the grill grates. Grill for about 2-3 minutes, or until grill marks appear and the avocados are slightly warmed through.
6. Serve:
    - Carefully remove the grilled avocados from the grill and transfer them to a serving platter or individual plates.
    - Serve immediately while warm. Optionally, top with salsa, chopped tomatoes, cilantro, a squeeze of lime juice, or a sprinkle of smoked paprika for added flavor.

Tips:

- Avocado ripeness: Use ripe avocados that give slightly to gentle pressure. They should be firm but yield to a gentle squeeze.
- Grill temperature: Medium-high heat works best for grilling avocados to achieve nice grill marks without overcooking.
- Variations: Experiment with different toppings and seasonings to suit your taste preferences. Grilled avocado pairs well with a variety of flavors, so feel free to get creative!

Grilled avocado is a versatile dish that can be enjoyed as a side, appetizer, or part of a larger meal. It's quick to prepare and adds a delicious twist to your grilling repertoire. Enjoy the creamy texture and subtle smokiness of grilled avocados!

BBQ Black Bean Burgers

Ingredients:

For the black bean burgers:

- 1 can (15 ounces) black beans, drained and rinsed
- 1/2 cup cooked quinoa (or substitute with breadcrumbs or oats)
- 1/4 cup finely chopped onion
- 2 cloves garlic, minced
- 1 tablespoon soy sauce or tamari
- 1 tablespoon tomato paste
- 1 teaspoon smoked paprika
- 1/2 teaspoon ground cumin
- Salt and pepper, to taste
- 1/4 cup barbecue sauce (choose a vegan variety)
- 1/4 cup breadcrumbs (gluten-free if needed)
- Oil for frying (such as olive oil or vegetable oil)

For assembling and serving:

- Burger buns (choose vegan buns if needed)
- Lettuce, tomato slices, onion slices, avocado slices, or any other toppings of choice
- Additional barbecue sauce, for serving

Instructions:

1. Prepare the black bean mixture:
    - In a large bowl, mash half of the black beans with a fork or potato masher until mostly smooth. Add the remaining whole black beans.
    - Add cooked quinoa (or breadcrumbs/oats), chopped onion, minced garlic, soy sauce or tamari, tomato paste, smoked paprika, ground cumin, salt, pepper, barbecue sauce, and breadcrumbs to the bowl. Mix well until everything is combined and the mixture holds together when pressed.
2. Form the burgers:
    - Divide the black bean mixture into 4 equal portions. Use your hands to shape each portion into a burger patty, about 1/2 to 3/4 inch thick.
3. Cook the burgers:
    - Heat a large skillet over medium heat and add enough oil to coat the bottom of the skillet.
    - Once the oil is hot, carefully place the burger patties in the skillet. Cook for about 4-5 minutes on each side, or until the burgers are golden brown and heated through. Add more oil if needed.
4. Assemble the burgers:
    - Toast the burger buns if desired. Place a black bean burger patty on the bottom half of each bun.

- Top each burger patty with lettuce, tomato slices, onion slices, avocado slices, or any other toppings of your choice.
- Drizzle additional barbecue sauce over the toppings if desired.
5. Serve:
    - Close the burgers with the top halves of the burger buns.
    - Serve the BBQ black bean burgers hot, with your favorite sides like sweet potato fries, coleslaw, or a fresh salad.

Tips:

- Burger consistency: If the mixture is too wet to form into patties, add more breadcrumbs or oats until it holds together. If it's too dry, add a little water or additional barbecue sauce.
- Grilling option: These burgers can also be grilled on a preheated grill. Brush the grill grates with oil and grill the burgers for about 4-5 minutes on each side, or until heated through and grill marks appear.
- Make-ahead: You can prepare the burger patties ahead of time and refrigerate them until ready to cook. This allows the flavors to meld together.

These BBQ black bean burgers are hearty, flavorful, and perfect for vegans and non-vegans alike. Enjoy the delicious combination of black beans, barbecue sauce, and savory seasonings in this satisfying burger!

Grilled Peaches

Ingredients:

For the black bean burgers:

- 1 can (15 ounces) black beans, drained and rinsed
- 1/2 cup cooked quinoa (or substitute with breadcrumbs or oats)
- 1/4 cup finely chopped onion
- 2 cloves garlic, minced
- 1 tablespoon soy sauce or tamari
- 1 tablespoon tomato paste
- 1 teaspoon smoked paprika
- 1/2 teaspoon ground cumin
- Salt and pepper, to taste
- 1/4 cup barbecue sauce (choose a vegan variety)
- 1/4 cup breadcrumbs (gluten-free if needed)
- Oil for frying (such as olive oil or vegetable oil)

For assembling and serving:

- Burger buns (choose vegan buns if needed)
- Lettuce, tomato slices, onion slices, avocado slices, or any other toppings of choice
- Additional barbecue sauce, for serving

Instructions:

1. Prepare the black bean mixture:
    - In a large bowl, mash half of the black beans with a fork or potato masher until mostly smooth. Add the remaining whole black beans.
    - Add cooked quinoa (or breadcrumbs/oats), chopped onion, minced garlic, soy sauce or tamari, tomato paste, smoked paprika, ground cumin, salt, pepper, barbecue sauce, and breadcrumbs to the bowl. Mix well until everything is combined and the mixture holds together when pressed.
2. Form the burgers:
    - Divide the black bean mixture into 4 equal portions. Use your hands to shape each portion into a burger patty, about 1/2 to 3/4 inch thick.
3. Cook the burgers:
    - Heat a large skillet over medium heat and add enough oil to coat the bottom of the skillet.
    - Once the oil is hot, carefully place the burger patties in the skillet. Cook for about 4-5 minutes on each side, or until the burgers are golden brown and heated through. Add more oil if needed.
4. Assemble the burgers:
    - Toast the burger buns if desired. Place a black bean burger patty on the bottom half of each bun.

- Top each burger patty with lettuce, tomato slices, onion slices, avocado slices, or any other toppings of your choice.
- Drizzle additional barbecue sauce over the toppings if desired.

5. Serve:
    - Close the burgers with the top halves of the burger buns.
    - Serve the BBQ black bean burgers hot, with your favorite sides like sweet potato fries, coleslaw, or a fresh salad.

Tips:

- Burger consistency: If the mixture is too wet to form into patties, add more breadcrumbs or oats until it holds together. If it's too dry, add a little water or additional barbecue sauce.
- Grilling option: These burgers can also be grilled on a preheated grill. Brush the grill grates with oil and grill the burgers for about 4-5 minutes on each side, or until heated through and grill marks appear.
- Make-ahead: You can prepare the burger patties ahead of time and refrigerate them until ready to cook. This allows the flavors to meld together.

These BBQ black bean burgers are hearty, flavorful, and perfect for vegans and non-vegans alike. Enjoy the delicious combination of black beans, barbecue sauce, and savory seasonings in this satisfying burger!

Grilled Peaches

Ingredients:

- 4 ripe peaches
- 2 tablespoons maple syrup or honey (for non-vegan option)
- 1 tablespoon olive oil
- 1/2 teaspoon ground cinnamon (optional)
- Pinch of salt
- Vanilla ice cream or Greek yogurt, for serving (optional)
- Fresh mint leaves, chopped (for garnish, optional)

Instructions:

1. Prepare the peaches:
   - Wash the peaches and pat them dry with a paper towel. Cut each peach in half and remove the pits.
2. Preheat the grill:
   - Preheat your grill to medium-high heat.
3. Prepare the marinade:
   - In a small bowl, whisk together the maple syrup or honey (if using), olive oil, ground cinnamon (if using), and a pinch of salt.
4. Grill the peaches:
   - Brush the cut sides of the peach halves generously with the marinade mixture.
   - Place the peaches cut-side down on the preheated grill.
   - Grill for about 3-4 minutes, or until grill marks appear and the peaches are slightly softened.
   - Carefully flip the peaches using tongs and grill for an additional 2-3 minutes on the skin side. The peaches should be tender but still hold their shape.
5. Serve:
   - Remove the grilled peaches from the grill and transfer them to a serving platter or individual plates.
   - Serve the grilled peaches warm. They can be enjoyed on their own, with a scoop of vanilla ice cream or Greek yogurt, or topped with a sprinkle of fresh mint leaves for garnish.

Tips:

- Peach ripeness: Use ripe but firm peaches for grilling. They should give slightly to gentle pressure without being too soft.
- Grill temperature: Medium-high heat is ideal for grilling peaches to achieve nice grill marks without overcooking.
- Variations: Experiment with different flavors by adding a pinch of ground nutmeg or ginger to the marinade. You can also drizzle the grilled peaches with a balsamic reduction or sprinkle with chopped nuts for added texture.

Grilled peaches are a simple yet elegant dessert or side dish that captures the essence of summer. Enjoy the sweet, smoky flavors of grilled peaches at your next barbecue or outdoor gathering!

BBQ Mushroom Sliders

Ingredients:

For the BBQ mushrooms:

- 1 pound cremini mushrooms, cleaned and sliced
- 1/2 cup barbecue sauce (choose a vegan variety)
- 2 tablespoons olive oil
- 2 cloves garlic, minced
- 1 teaspoon smoked paprika
- Salt and pepper, to taste

For assembling the sliders:

- Slider buns or small hamburger buns (choose vegan buns if needed)
- Coleslaw or shredded lettuce
- Sliced tomatoes
- Sliced red onions
- Pickles (optional)

Instructions:

1. Prepare the BBQ mushrooms:
   - In a bowl, whisk together the barbecue sauce, olive oil, minced garlic, smoked paprika, salt, and pepper.
   - Add the sliced mushrooms to the bowl and toss gently until they are well coated with the marinade. Let them marinate for at least 15-30 minutes to absorb the flavors.
2. Cook the mushrooms:
   - Heat a large skillet or grill pan over medium-high heat. If using an outdoor grill, preheat it to medium-high heat.
   - Add the marinated mushrooms to the skillet or grill pan in a single layer, ensuring they are not overcrowded.
   - Cook the mushrooms for about 5-7 minutes, stirring occasionally, until they are tender and slightly caramelized. Adjust the heat as needed to prevent burning.
3. Assemble the sliders:
   - Toast the slider buns lightly if desired.
   - Place a generous amount of BBQ mushrooms on the bottom half of each bun.
   - Top with coleslaw or shredded lettuce, sliced tomatoes, sliced red onions, and pickles if using.
   - Place the top half of the bun on top of the toppings to complete the sliders.
4. Serve:
   - Arrange the BBQ Mushroom Sliders on a platter and serve immediately while warm.

Tips:

- Mushroom selection: Cremini mushrooms work well for their meaty texture, but you can also use button mushrooms or portobello mushrooms for a different flavor profile.
- Slider variations: Customize the sliders with your favorite toppings such as avocado slices, vegan cheese, or different types of sauces.
- Grilling option: You can grill the marinated mushrooms on a preheated grill instead of using a skillet. Use a grill basket or skewers to prevent the mushrooms from falling through the grates.

These BBQ Mushroom Sliders are flavorful, hearty, and perfect for a vegetarian or vegan meal option. They're sure to be a hit at your next barbecue or party! Enjoy the delicious combination of BBQ mushrooms and fresh toppings in every bite.

Grilled Bell Peppers

Ingredients:

- 3-4 bell peppers (red, yellow, and/or green)
- 2 tablespoons olive oil
- Salt and pepper, to taste
- Optional: Balsamic vinegar, fresh herbs (such as parsley or basil), garlic powder, or crushed red pepper flakes for seasoning

Instructions:

1. Prepare the bell peppers:
    - Wash the bell peppers and pat them dry with a paper towel. Cut each bell pepper in half lengthwise and remove the stems, seeds, and white membranes.
2. Preheat the grill:
    - Preheat your grill to medium-high heat.
3. Grill the bell peppers:
    - Brush both sides of the bell pepper halves with olive oil and season with salt and pepper. If desired, you can also drizzle a little balsamic vinegar over the peppers for added flavor.
    - Place the bell pepper halves on the preheated grill, cut-side down.
    - Grill for about 4-5 minutes, or until the peppers have grill marks and are starting to soften.
    - Flip the bell pepper halves using tongs and grill for an additional 3-4 minutes on the other side, until they are tender and lightly charred.
4. Serve:
    - Remove the grilled bell peppers from the grill and transfer them to a serving platter.
    - Optionally, sprinkle with fresh herbs, garlic powder, or crushed red pepper flakes for added flavor.
    - Serve the grilled bell peppers hot as a side dish, or use them as toppings for sandwiches, salads, or pasta dishes.

Tips:

- Bell pepper selection: Choose firm and brightly colored bell peppers for the best flavor and texture. Red, yellow, and orange bell peppers tend to be sweeter when grilled.
- Grill temperature: Medium-high heat works well for grilling bell peppers to achieve nice grill marks without overcooking.
- Variations: Experiment with different seasonings and herbs to suit your taste preferences. You can also grill whole bell peppers instead of halves, then slice them after grilling.

Grilled bell peppers are not only delicious but also packed with vitamins and antioxidants. Enjoy their smoky-sweet flavor and tender texture as a versatile addition to your meals!

BBQ Soy Curls

Ingredients:

- 1 package (8-10 ounces) soy curls
- 1 cup vegetable broth or water
- 1/2 cup barbecue sauce (choose a vegan variety)
- 2 tablespoons soy sauce or tamari
- 2 tablespoons maple syrup or agave syrup
- 1 tablespoon olive oil
- 1 teaspoon smoked paprika
- 1/2 teaspoon garlic powder
- Salt and pepper, to taste

Instructions:

1. Prepare the soy curls:
    - Place the soy curls in a large bowl and cover them with vegetable broth or water. Let them soak for about 10-15 minutes, or until they are fully rehydrated and softened.
2. Drain and squeeze out excess liquid:
    - Drain the rehydrated soy curls and gently squeeze them to remove excess liquid. You want them to be moist but not dripping.
3. Marinate the soy curls:
    - In a bowl, whisk together barbecue sauce, soy sauce or tamari, maple syrup or agave syrup, olive oil, smoked paprika, garlic powder, salt, and pepper.
    - Add the rehydrated soy curls to the marinade and toss until they are evenly coated. Let them marinate for at least 15-20 minutes to absorb the flavors.
4. Cook the BBQ Soy Curls:
    - Heat a large skillet or grill pan over medium-high heat. If using an outdoor grill, preheat it to medium-high heat.
    - Add the marinated soy curls to the skillet or grill pan in a single layer. Cook for about 8-10 minutes, stirring occasionally, until the soy curls are heated through and slightly caramelized. Adjust the heat as needed to prevent burning.
5. Serve:
    - Remove the BBQ Soy Curls from the heat and transfer them to a serving dish.
    - Serve hot as a main dish, in sandwiches or wraps, or as a topping for salads.

Tips:

- Soy curl texture: Ensure the soy curls are fully rehydrated and properly drained before cooking to achieve the best texture.
- Barbecue sauce: Use your favorite vegan barbecue sauce or make your own. Adjust the sweetness and spiciness according to your taste preferences.
- Variations: Customize the marinade with additional spices such as cumin, chili powder, or a dash of hot sauce for extra heat.

BBQ Soy Curls are a flavorful and protein-packed option for vegans and vegetarians, offering a satisfying BBQ experience without meat. Enjoy them in various dishes or as a standalone meal!

Grilled Tofu Steaks

Ingredients:

- 1 block (14-16 ounces) extra-firm tofu
- 1/4 cup soy sauce or tamari
- 2 tablespoons olive oil
- 2 tablespoons maple syrup or agave syrup
- 2 cloves garlic, minced
- 1 teaspoon smoked paprika
- 1/2 teaspoon ground cumin
- 1/2 teaspoon onion powder
- Salt and pepper, to taste
- Optional: Fresh herbs (such as cilantro or parsley) for garnish

Instructions:

1. Prepare the tofu:
   - Press the tofu to remove excess moisture: Place the block of tofu between two plates lined with paper towels or a clean kitchen towel. Place a heavy object (like a cast iron skillet or cans of food) on top of the tofu and let it press for at least 15-20 minutes. This step helps the tofu absorb flavors better and achieve a firmer texture.
2. Prepare the marinade:
   - In a shallow dish or bowl, whisk together soy sauce or tamari, olive oil, maple syrup or agave syrup, minced garlic, smoked paprika, ground cumin, onion powder, salt, and pepper.
3. Marinate the tofu:
   - Cut the pressed tofu block into 4 equal-sized steaks (about 1/2 to 3/4 inch thick).
   - Place the tofu steaks in the marinade, ensuring they are well coated on all sides. Let them marinate for at least 30 minutes to 1 hour, flipping them halfway through to ensure even marination.
4. Grill the tofu steaks:
   - Preheat your grill to medium-high heat. Alternatively, you can use a grill pan on the stovetop.
   - Lightly oil the grill grates or grill pan to prevent sticking.
   - Carefully place the tofu steaks on the preheated grill or grill pan. Reserve the marinade for basting.
   - Grill the tofu steaks for about 5-7 minutes on each side, or until they have nice grill marks and are heated through. Baste with the remaining marinade while grilling to enhance flavor.
5. Serve:
   - Remove the grilled tofu steaks from the grill and transfer them to a serving platter.
   - Garnish with fresh herbs if desired.

- Serve hot as a main dish, accompanied by your favorite sides such as grilled vegetables, rice, or salad.

Tips:

- Tofu selection: Extra-firm tofu works best for grilling as it holds its shape well and has a firmer texture.
- Grill temperature: Medium-high heat is ideal for grilling tofu steaks to achieve nice grill marks without overcooking.
- Variations: Customize the marinade with additional spices or herbs, such as ginger, chili flakes, or thyme, to suit your taste preferences.
- Presentation: For an added touch, serve grilled tofu steaks with a squeeze of fresh lemon or lime juice, or a drizzle of balsamic glaze.

Grilled tofu steaks are a healthy, protein-rich dish that's perfect for vegans and vegetarians, or anyone looking to enjoy a flavorful grilled meal. Enjoy the deliciously marinated tofu with its smoky flavor and tender texture!

BBQ Chickpea Salad

Ingredients:

For the BBQ Chickpeas:

- 1 can (15 ounces) chickpeas, drained and rinsed
- 1/4 cup barbecue sauce (choose a vegan variety)
- 1 tablespoon olive oil
- 1/2 teaspoon smoked paprika
- Salt and pepper, to taste

For the Salad:

- Mixed greens (lettuce, spinach, arugula, etc.)
- Cherry tomatoes, halved
- Cucumber, sliced
- Red onion, thinly sliced
- Avocado, sliced or diced
- Optional: Corn kernels, bell peppers, shredded carrots, or any other vegetables of choice

For the Dressing:

- 3 tablespoons olive oil
- 2 tablespoons apple cider vinegar or lemon juice
- 1 tablespoon maple syrup or honey (for non-vegan option)
- 1 teaspoon Dijon mustard
- 1 clove garlic, minced
- Salt and pepper, to taste

Instructions:

1. Prepare the BBQ Chickpeas:
    - Preheat your oven to 400°F (200°C).
    - In a bowl, combine the drained and rinsed chickpeas with barbecue sauce, olive oil, smoked paprika, salt, and pepper. Toss until the chickpeas are evenly coated.
    - Spread the chickpeas in a single layer on a baking sheet lined with parchment paper or aluminum foil.
    - Bake in the preheated oven for 20-25 minutes, stirring halfway through, until the chickpeas are crispy and slightly caramelized. Remove from the oven and set aside to cool slightly.
2. Prepare the Salad:
    - In a large salad bowl, combine mixed greens, cherry tomatoes, cucumber slices, red onion slices, avocado slices or cubes, and any other vegetables you like.
3. Make the Dressing:

- In a small bowl or jar, whisk together olive oil, apple cider vinegar or lemon juice, maple syrup or honey (if using), Dijon mustard, minced garlic, salt, and pepper until well combined.
4. Assemble the Salad:
    - Add the BBQ chickpeas to the salad bowl with the mixed greens and vegetables.
    - Drizzle the dressing over the salad and gently toss to coat everything evenly.
5. Serve:
    - Divide the BBQ Chickpea Salad into individual serving bowls or plates.
    - Optionally, garnish with fresh herbs, such as chopped parsley or cilantro.
    - Serve immediately and enjoy!

Tips:

- **Chickpea texture:** Ensure the chickpeas are well coated with the barbecue sauce mixture before baking to achieve a crispy texture.
- **Salad variations:** Feel free to customize the salad with your favorite vegetables or add additional protein sources such as grilled tofu, tempeh, or nuts.
- **Make-ahead:** You can prepare the BBQ chickpeas and dressing ahead of time and store them separately in the refrigerator. Assemble the salad just before serving to maintain freshness.

This BBQ Chickpea Salad is not only nutritious but also bursting with flavors and textures. It's perfect for a light lunch or dinner, and the BBQ chickpeas add a satisfying crunch and smoky taste. Enjoy this refreshing salad with your favorite summer vegetables!

Grilled Tomato Bruschetta

Ingredients:

- 4-5 ripe tomatoes, diced
- 1-2 cloves of garlic, minced
- Fresh basil leaves, chopped
- 1 tablespoon balsamic vinegar
- 2 tablespoons extra virgin olive oil
- Salt and pepper to taste
- Baguette or Italian bread, sliced
- Olive oil for brushing

Instructions:

1. Prepare the tomatoes: In a bowl, combine the diced tomatoes, minced garlic, chopped basil leaves, balsamic vinegar, olive oil, salt, and pepper. Mix well and let it marinate for at least 15-20 minutes to allow the flavors to meld together.
2. Grill the bread: Preheat a grill or grill pan over medium-high heat. Brush the bread slices with olive oil on both sides. Grill each side for about 1-2 minutes or until nicely toasted with grill marks.
3. Assemble the bruschetta: Once the bread slices are grilled, spoon the tomato mixture generously over each slice.
4. Serve: Arrange the bruschetta on a platter and serve immediately while the bread is still warm and crisp.

Tips:

- Use ripe, flavorful tomatoes for the best results.
- You can adjust the amount of garlic, basil, and vinegar according to your taste preferences.
- If you don't have a grill, you can toast the bread in a toaster or oven.
- Drizzle a little extra olive oil on top before serving for added richness.

Enjoy your Grilled Tomato Bruschetta as a tasty appetizer or snack!

BBQ Cauliflower Steaks

Ingredients:

- 1 large head of cauliflower
- 1 cup BBQ sauce (homemade or store-bought)
- 2 tablespoons olive oil
- 1 teaspoon smoked paprika
- 1/2 teaspoon garlic powder
- Salt and pepper, to taste
- Fresh parsley or cilantro, chopped (optional, for garnish)

Instructions:

1. Prepare the cauliflower: Remove the outer leaves from the cauliflower and trim the stem end so it sits flat on the cutting board. Cut the cauliflower into thick slices (about 1-inch thick), aiming to keep the slices intact. These slices are your "cauliflower steaks."
2. Marinate the cauliflower: In a bowl, whisk together the BBQ sauce, olive oil, smoked paprika, garlic powder, salt, and pepper. Brush both sides of each cauliflower steak generously with the marinade. Allow the cauliflower to marinate for at least 15-20 minutes to absorb the flavors.
3. Grill the cauliflower: Preheat your grill to medium-high heat. Place the cauliflower steaks on the grill and cook for about 5-7 minutes on each side, or until they are tender and nicely charred, basting with the remaining marinade as they cook.
4. Serve: Once grilled, transfer the cauliflower steaks to a serving platter. Garnish with chopped parsley or cilantro if desired. Serve hot and enjoy!

Tips:

- Make sure your cauliflower steaks are thick enough to hold together on the grill.
- Adjust the grilling time based on the thickness of your cauliflower steaks and your desired level of tenderness.
- You can also roast the cauliflower steaks in the oven if you don't have a grill. Preheat the oven to 425°F (220°C) and roast for about 20-25 minutes, flipping once halfway through, until tender and caramelized.

BBQ Cauliflower Steaks are a flavorful and hearty dish that's sure to be a hit, whether you're serving vegetarians or meat-eaters alike!

Grilled Watermelon

Ingredients:

- 1 small seedless watermelon, cut into wedges or slices
- Olive oil or vegetable oil, for brushing
- Salt (optional)
- Fresh mint leaves, chopped (optional, for garnish)
- Balsamic glaze or reduction (optional, for drizzling)

Instructions:

1. Prepare the grill: Preheat your grill to medium-high heat.
2. Prepare the watermelon: Cut the watermelon into wedges or slices, ensuring they are about 1 inch thick. Remove any seeds if necessary.
3. Brush with oil: Lightly brush both sides of each watermelon slice with olive oil or vegetable oil. This helps to prevent sticking and promotes even grilling.
4. Grill the watermelon: Place the watermelon slices directly onto the grill grates. Grill for about 2-3 minutes on each side, or until grill marks appear and the watermelon caramelizes slightly. Avoid overcooking as you want the watermelon to remain firm yet slightly tender.
5. Serve: Remove the grilled watermelon slices from the grill and arrange them on a serving platter. Sprinkle lightly with salt if desired. Optionally, garnish with chopped fresh mint leaves and drizzle with balsamic glaze or reduction for added flavor.
6. Enjoy: Serve the grilled watermelon slices immediately while they are still warm from the grill. They can be enjoyed as a refreshing appetizer or side dish.

Tips:

- Make sure your grill is clean and well-oiled to prevent the watermelon from sticking.
- Experiment with different seasonings like a sprinkle of chili powder or a squeeze of lime juice for added flavor.
- Grilled watermelon pairs well with savory ingredients like feta cheese or a dash of black pepper for a contrast of flavors.

Grilled watermelon is a unique and tasty treat that adds a smoky sweetness to your summer meals. It's sure to impress your guests at your next barbecue or outdoor gathering!

BBQ Seitan Ribs

Ingredients:

- 1 cup vital wheat gluten flour
- 2 tablespoons nutritional yeast
- 1 teaspoon smoked paprika
- 1 teaspoon garlic powder
- 1/2 teaspoon onion powder
- 1/2 teaspoon salt
- 1/2 teaspoon black pepper
- 3/4 cup vegetable broth
- 2 tablespoons soy sauce or tamari
- 2 tablespoons tomato paste
- 1 tablespoon olive oil
- BBQ sauce of your choice

Instructions:

1. Prepare the seitan dough: In a mixing bowl, combine the vital wheat gluten flour, nutritional yeast, smoked paprika, garlic powder, onion powder, salt, and black pepper.
2. Make the seitan dough: In a separate bowl, whisk together the vegetable broth, soy sauce or tamari, tomato paste, and olive oil. Pour the wet ingredients into the dry ingredients and stir until well combined and a dough forms.
3. Knead the dough: Turn the dough out onto a clean surface and knead for about 3-5 minutes until it becomes elastic and springs back when pressed. Let the dough rest for 5-10 minutes.
4. Shape the ribs: Divide the dough into 4-6 equal portions, depending on how large you want your ribs to be. Shape each portion into a flat rectangular shape, resembling rib shapes.
5. Steam the ribs: Prepare a steamer basket or a pot with a steamer insert. Steam the seitan ribs for 30-40 minutes, flipping halfway through, until they are firm and cooked through.
6. Grill the ribs: Preheat your grill to medium-high heat. Brush each seitan rib generously with BBQ sauce on both sides.
7. Grill the ribs: Place the ribs on the grill and cook for about 3-4 minutes on each side, brushing with additional BBQ sauce as needed, until they are nicely caramelized and heated through.
8. Serve: Remove the BBQ Seitan Ribs from the grill and serve hot. They pair well with coleslaw, cornbread, or your favorite barbecue sides.

Tips:

- Ensure the seitan dough is well-kneaded to develop its texture.
- Adjust the seasonings in the dough to suit your taste preferences.
- Use your favorite BBQ sauce for basting and serving.

- If you don't have a grill, you can bake the ribs in the oven at 375°F (190°C) for 20-25 minutes after steaming, brushing with BBQ sauce halfway through.

Enjoy these BBQ Seitan Ribs as a delicious and satisfying vegan alternative that's perfect for summer cookouts or any time you're craving barbecue flavors!

Grilled Portobello Burgers

Ingredients:

- 4 large portobello mushroom caps, stems removed
- 2 tablespoons balsamic vinegar
- 2 tablespoons soy sauce or tamari
- 2 tablespoons olive oil
- 2 cloves garlic, minced
- 1 teaspoon dried oregano
- Salt and pepper, to taste
- Burger buns
- Burger toppings of your choice (lettuce, tomato, onion, avocado, cheese, etc.)
- Optional: additional marinade or BBQ sauce for basting

Instructions:

1. Prepare the marinade: In a small bowl, whisk together the balsamic vinegar, soy sauce or tamari, olive oil, minced garlic, dried oregano, salt, and pepper.
2. Marinate the mushrooms: Place the portobello mushroom caps in a shallow dish or a large zip-top bag. Pour the marinade over the mushrooms, making sure they are well coated. Let them marinate for at least 30 minutes, flipping them halfway through to ensure even marination.
3. Preheat the grill: Preheat your grill to medium-high heat.
4. Grill the mushrooms: Remove the mushrooms from the marinade and place them on the grill, gill side down. Grill for about 4-5 minutes on each side, or until they are tender and grill marks appear. Optionally, brush them with additional marinade or BBQ sauce while grilling for extra flavor.
5. Toast the buns: While the mushrooms are grilling, lightly toast the burger buns on the grill until they are warm and slightly crisp.
6. Assemble the burgers: Place each grilled portobello mushroom cap on a toasted bun. Add your favorite burger toppings such as lettuce, tomato, onion, avocado, cheese, or any condiments you like.
7. Serve: Serve the Grilled Portobello Burgers immediately while they are warm and enjoy!

Tips:

- Choose large and firm portobello mushroom caps for best results.
- You can add cheese slices to the mushrooms during the last minute of grilling for a melty topping.
- Customize your burger toppings to your preference for a personalized touch.
- If you don't have a grill, you can also cook the mushrooms in a grill pan on the stovetop or bake them in the oven at 400°F (200°C) for about 15-20 minutes.

Grilled Portobello Burgers are a delicious and satisfying vegetarian option that's sure to please everyone at your next barbecue or summer gathering!

BBQ Lentil Meatballs

Ingredients:

For the Lentil Meatballs:

- 1 cup dried brown lentils
- 2 cups vegetable broth or water
- 1/2 cup breadcrumbs (regular or gluten-free)
- 1/4 cup grated Parmesan cheese (optional, omit for vegan version)
- 2 cloves garlic, minced
- 1 teaspoon dried oregano
- 1 teaspoon dried basil
- 1/2 teaspoon smoked paprika
- Salt and pepper, to taste
- 1 tablespoon olive oil (for cooking)

For the BBQ Sauce:

- 1 cup BBQ sauce of your choice (homemade or store-bought)
- 2 tablespoons tomato paste
- 1 tablespoon soy sauce or tamari
- 1 tablespoon maple syrup or brown sugar
- 1 teaspoon apple cider vinegar
- 1/2 teaspoon smoked paprika
- Salt and pepper, to taste

Instructions:

1. Cook the lentils: Rinse the lentils thoroughly under cold water. In a medium saucepan, bring the vegetable broth or water to a boil. Add the lentils, reduce the heat to low, cover, and simmer for about 20-25 minutes, or until the lentils are tender and most of the liquid is absorbed. Drain any excess liquid and let the lentils cool slightly.
2. Prepare the BBQ sauce: In a small saucepan, combine all the BBQ sauce ingredients - BBQ sauce, tomato paste, soy sauce or tamari, maple syrup or brown sugar, apple cider vinegar, smoked paprika, salt, and pepper. Simmer over low heat for 5-7 minutes, stirring occasionally, until the sauce is slightly thickened. Remove from heat and set aside.
3. Make the lentil mixture: In a large mixing bowl, mash the cooked lentils with a fork or potato masher until they are mostly broken down. Add the breadcrumbs, grated Parmesan cheese (if using), minced garlic, dried oregano, dried basil, smoked paprika, salt, and pepper. Mix well until combined. If the mixture seems too dry, you can add a tablespoon or two of water or vegetable broth to moisten it.
4. Form the meatballs: Preheat your oven to 375°F (190°C) and line a baking sheet with parchment paper. Take about 1-2 tablespoons of the lentil mixture and roll it into a ball between your palms. Place each meatball on the prepared baking sheet. Repeat until all the mixture is used, making approximately 20-24 meatballs.
5. Bake the meatballs: Bake the lentil meatballs in the preheated oven for 20-25 minutes, or until they are golden brown and firm to the touch.

6. Coat with BBQ sauce: Remove the meatballs from the oven and transfer them to a large mixing bowl. Pour the BBQ sauce over the meatballs and gently toss to coat them evenly.
7. Serve: Arrange the BBQ Lentil Meatballs on a serving platter or plate. Optionally, garnish with chopped fresh parsley or green onions. Serve warm and enjoy!

Tips:

- You can prepare the lentil meatballs ahead of time and store them in the refrigerator until ready to bake and coat with BBQ sauce.
- Adjust the seasoning and sweetness of the BBQ sauce to your taste preference.
- These BBQ Lentil Meatballs are great served as appetizers with toothpicks for dipping or as a main course with a side of rice or salad.

BBQ Lentil Meatballs are a delicious and nutritious vegetarian dish that's packed with protein and flavor, perfect for any occasion!

Grilled Baby Potatoes

Ingredients:

- 1 lb baby potatoes, washed and halved (you can use any small variety like fingerling, new potatoes, or Yukon gold)
- 2-3 tablespoons olive oil
- 2 cloves garlic, minced (optional)
- 1 teaspoon dried thyme
- 1 teaspoon dried rosemary
- Salt and pepper, to taste
- Fresh parsley, chopped (optional, for garnish)

Instructions:

1. Preheat the grill: Preheat your grill to medium-high heat.
2. Prepare the potatoes: Wash and halve the baby potatoes. If they are larger, you can quarter them to ensure even cooking.
3. Season the potatoes: In a large bowl, toss the halved potatoes with olive oil, minced garlic (if using), dried thyme, dried rosemary, salt, and pepper. Make sure the potatoes are evenly coated with the seasoning.
4. Grill the potatoes: Place the seasoned potatoes directly on the grill grate, cut side down. Close the grill lid and cook for about 10-15 minutes, or until the potatoes are tender and golden brown, stirring occasionally to ensure even cooking.
5. Serve: Once the potatoes are grilled to perfection, transfer them to a serving dish. Garnish with chopped fresh parsley if desired and serve hot.

Tips:

- Parboiling option: For faster cooking, you can parboil the baby potatoes for about 5-7 minutes before grilling. This ensures they cook through evenly on the grill.
- Grill basket: If you're concerned about the potatoes falling through the grill grates, you can use a grill basket or skewer them on metal skewers.
- Variations: Feel free to customize the seasoning with your favorite herbs and spices. You can also add a sprinkle of paprika or chili flakes for some heat.

Grilled baby potatoes are a versatile and delicious addition to any barbecue or summer meal. They're easy to prepare and are sure to be a hit with everyone!

BBQ Tempeh Sandwiches

Ingredients:

For the BBQ Tempeh:

- 1 package (8 oz) tempeh, cut into thin strips or triangles
- 1 cup BBQ sauce of your choice (homemade or store-bought)
- 2 tablespoons olive oil
- 1 tablespoon soy sauce or tamari
- 1 tablespoon maple syrup or brown sugar
- 1 teaspoon smoked paprika
- 1/2 teaspoon garlic powder
- Salt and pepper, to taste

For the Sandwiches:

- Burger buns or sandwich rolls
- Coleslaw (optional, for topping)
- Sliced red onion (optional, for topping)
- Pickles (optional, for topping)

Instructions:

1. Prepare the BBQ Tempeh:
   - In a mixing bowl, whisk together the BBQ sauce, olive oil, soy sauce or tamari, maple syrup or brown sugar, smoked paprika, garlic powder, salt, and pepper.
   - Add the tempeh strips to the bowl and toss gently to coat them evenly with the marinade. Let the tempeh marinate for at least 15-20 minutes, or longer if time permits.
2. Cook the BBQ Tempeh:
   - Heat a large skillet or grill pan over medium-high heat. Add the marinated tempeh strips (reserve the marinade) and cook for 3-4 minutes on each side, or until they are caramelized and heated through. You can also grill the tempeh strips on an outdoor grill for a smokier flavor.
3. Simmer the marinade (optional):
   - If desired, pour the reserved marinade into a small saucepan and simmer over low heat for 5-7 minutes, until it thickens slightly. This can be used as an additional sauce for the sandwiches.
4. Assemble the sandwiches:
   - Toast the burger buns or sandwich rolls lightly.
   - Place a generous amount of BBQ tempeh strips on the bottom half of each bun.
   - Top with coleslaw, sliced red onion, pickles, or any other toppings you prefer.
   - Drizzle with the simmered marinade or additional BBQ sauce if desired.
5. Serve:
   - Close the sandwiches with the top half of the buns and serve immediately while warm.

Tips:

- Marinating time: Allowing the tempeh to marinate enhances its flavor. You can prepare the marinade ahead of time and marinate the tempeh overnight for even more flavor.
- Texture: For a firmer texture, steam the tempeh for 10 minutes before marinating and cooking. This helps remove any bitterness and allows the tempeh to absorb the flavors better.
- Customization: Feel free to customize the sandwiches with your favorite toppings and condiments. Avocado slices, fresh greens, or a slice of vegan cheese can also be great additions.

BBQ Tempeh Sandwiches are a delicious and nutritious meal that's sure to satisfy both vegetarians and meat-eaters alike. Enjoy them for lunch, dinner, or at your next barbecue gathering!

Grilled Radicchio

Ingredients:

- 1 head of radicchio

- Olive oil
- Balsamic vinegar (optional)
- Salt and pepper, to taste
- Fresh herbs like thyme or rosemary (optional, for garnish)

Instructions:

1. Prepare the radicchio:
   - Cut the radicchio head into quarters, leaving the core intact to hold the leaves together.
2. Preheat the grill:
   - Preheat your grill to medium-high heat.
3. Brush with oil:
   - Brush both sides of each radicchio quarter lightly with olive oil. This helps prevent sticking and promotes even grilling.
4. Grill the radicchio:
   - Place the radicchio quarters on the grill, cut side down. Grill for about 3-4 minutes per side, or until they are slightly charred and tender when pierced with a fork.
5. Season:
   - Remove the grilled radicchio from the grill and season with salt and pepper to taste. Optionally, drizzle with a little balsamic vinegar for added flavor.
6. Serve:
   - Arrange the grilled radicchio quarters on a serving platter. Garnish with fresh herbs like thyme or rosemary if desired.

Tips:

- Handling radicchio: Radicchio can be quite sturdy, but grilling will soften it. Keep an eye on it to prevent burning, especially since it cooks relatively quickly.
- Variations: You can experiment with different seasonings such as garlic powder, lemon zest, or a sprinkle of Parmesan cheese after grilling.
- Pairings: Grilled radicchio is excellent served alongside grilled meats, seafood, or as part of a vegetarian platter. It also adds a unique touch to salads when chopped and mixed with other greens.

Grilled radicchio makes for a flavorful and visually appealing side dish that's easy to prepare and sure to impress at your next barbecue or dinner gathering!

BBQ Chickpea Kebabs

Ingredients:

- 1 can (15 oz) chickpeas, drained and rinsed
- 1 red bell pepper, cut into chunks

- 1 red onion, cut into chunks
- 1 zucchini, sliced
- 1/4 cup BBQ sauce (homemade or store-bought)
- 2 tablespoons olive oil
- 1 tablespoon soy sauce or tamari
- 1 tablespoon maple syrup or honey
- 1 teaspoon smoked paprika
- 1/2 teaspoon garlic powder
- Salt and pepper, to taste
- Wooden or metal skewers

Instructions:

1. Prepare the marinade: In a bowl, whisk together the BBQ sauce, olive oil, soy sauce or tamari, maple syrup or honey, smoked paprika, garlic powder, salt, and pepper.
2. Prepare the kebabs: Thread the chickpeas, red bell pepper chunks, red onion chunks, and zucchini slices onto skewers, alternating the ingredients as you go. Place the assembled kebabs in a shallow dish or on a tray.
3. Marinate the kebabs: Brush the BBQ marinade generously over the kebabs, making sure all sides are coated. Allow them to marinate for at least 15-20 minutes, or longer if time permits. Reserve some marinade for basting during grilling.
4. Preheat the grill: Preheat your grill to medium-high heat. If using wooden skewers, soak them in water for 20-30 minutes beforehand to prevent burning.
5. Grill the kebabs: Place the marinated kebabs on the grill. Grill for about 10-12 minutes, turning occasionally and basting with the reserved marinade, until the vegetables are tender and slightly charred.
6. Serve: Remove the BBQ Chickpea Kebabs from the grill and transfer them to a serving platter. Serve hot, garnished with fresh herbs if desired.

Tips:

- Vegetable options: Feel free to customize the kebabs with your favorite vegetables such as cherry tomatoes, mushrooms, or eggplant.
- Protein addition: For added protein, you can alternate chickpeas with cubes of firm tofu or seitan on the kebabs.
- Oven option: If you don't have a grill, you can bake the kebabs in the oven at 400°F (200°C) for 20-25 minutes, turning halfway through and basting with marinade.

BBQ Chickpea Kebabs are a tasty and nutritious vegetarian option that's perfect for summer grilling or any time you're craving flavorful skewers!

Grilled Stuffed Peppers

Ingredients:

- 4 large bell peppers (any color), tops cut off and seeds removed
- 1 cup quinoa, rinsed
- 2 cups vegetable broth or water

- 1 tablespoon olive oil
- 1 onion, finely chopped
- 2 cloves garlic, minced
- 1 zucchini, diced
- 1 carrot, diced
- 1/2 cup corn kernels (fresh or frozen)
- 1/2 cup black beans, drained and rinsed
- 1 teaspoon ground cumin
- 1 teaspoon smoked paprika
- Salt and pepper, to taste
- 1 cup shredded cheese (cheddar, mozzarella, or your choice)
- Fresh cilantro or parsley, chopped (optional, for garnish)

Instructions:

1. Prepare the quinoa: In a medium saucepan, bring the vegetable broth or water to a boil. Add the quinoa, reduce heat to low, cover, and simmer for 15-20 minutes, or until the liquid is absorbed and the quinoa is tender. Remove from heat and let it sit covered for 5 minutes. Fluff with a fork and set aside.
2. Prepare the peppers: Cut the tops off the bell peppers and remove the seeds and membranes. Rinse them under cold water and pat dry with paper towels.
3. Prepare the filling: In a large skillet, heat olive oil over medium heat. Add chopped onion and garlic, and sauté until softened, about 3-4 minutes. Add diced zucchini, carrot, corn kernels, black beans, ground cumin, smoked paprika, salt, and pepper. Cook for another 5-7 minutes, stirring occasionally, until the vegetables are tender.
4. Combine filling with quinoa: Add the cooked quinoa to the skillet with the vegetables. Stir to combine well. Taste and adjust seasoning if needed.
5. Stuff the peppers: Preheat your grill to medium-high heat. Stuff each bell pepper with the quinoa and vegetable mixture, packing it tightly. Top each stuffed pepper with shredded cheese.
6. Grill the stuffed peppers: Place the stuffed peppers on the grill, either directly on the grates or in a grill basket to prevent them from toppling over. Close the grill lid and cook for 15-20 minutes, or until the peppers are tender and the cheese is melted and bubbly.
7. Serve: Remove the grilled stuffed peppers from the grill and garnish with chopped fresh cilantro or parsley if desired. Serve hot and enjoy!

Tips:

- Variations: You can customize the filling by adding other vegetables like mushrooms, spinach, or tomatoes. You can also add protein such as cooked ground meat, tofu, or additional beans.
- Grill temperature: Monitor the grill temperature to ensure the peppers cook evenly without burning. Adjust the heat as needed.

- Make-ahead: You can prepare the filling and stuff the peppers ahead of time. Keep them covered in the refrigerator until ready to grill.

Grilled stuffed peppers are a flavorful and nutritious dish that's perfect for a vegetarian main course or a hearty side dish at your next barbecue or summer gathering!

BBQ Black Eyed Pea Burgers

Ingredients:

- 2 cans (15 oz each) black eyed peas, drained and rinsed

- 1/2 cup breadcrumbs (regular or gluten-free)
- 1/4 cup finely chopped onion
- 2 cloves garlic, minced
- 1 tablespoon BBQ sauce (plus extra for serving)
- 1 tablespoon soy sauce or tamari
- 1 teaspoon smoked paprika
- 1/2 teaspoon cumin
- Salt and pepper, to taste
- 2 tablespoons olive oil (for cooking)
- Burger buns
- Burger toppings of your choice (lettuce, tomato, onion, avocado, cheese, etc.)

Instructions:

1. Mash the black eyed peas: In a large bowl, mash the black eyed peas with a fork or potato masher until mostly smooth, leaving some texture.
2. Add the ingredients: Add the breadcrumbs, finely chopped onion, minced garlic, BBQ sauce, soy sauce or tamari, smoked paprika, cumin, salt, and pepper to the mashed black eyed peas. Mix well until all ingredients are combined.
3. Form the burger patties: Divide the mixture into 4-6 equal portions, depending on how large you want your burgers. Shape each portion into a patty about 1/2 to 3/4 inch thick.
4. Cook the burgers: Heat olive oil in a large skillet over medium heat. Once hot, add the burger patties to the skillet (you may need to cook them in batches depending on the size of your skillet). Cook for about 4-5 minutes on each side, or until the burgers are golden brown and heated through.
5. Prepare the buns: While the burgers are cooking, lightly toast the burger buns on the grill or in a toaster oven.
6. Assemble the burgers: Place each black eyed pea burger on a toasted bun. Add your favorite burger toppings such as lettuce, tomato, onion, avocado, cheese, or any condiments you like. Drizzle with extra BBQ sauce if desired.
7. Serve: Serve the BBQ Black Eyed Pea Burgers immediately while they are warm.

Tips:

- Texture: If the mixture feels too wet, add more breadcrumbs until you achieve a consistency that holds together well.
- Grilling option: You can also grill these burgers instead of cooking them in a skillet. Preheat your grill to medium-high heat and grill the burgers for about 4-5 minutes on each side, or until they have nice grill marks and are heated through.
- Make-ahead: You can prepare the burger patties ahead of time and refrigerate them until ready to cook. This allows the flavors to meld together.

BBQ Black Eyed Pea Burgers are a tasty and satisfying vegetarian option that's perfect for a barbecue or anytime you're craving a hearty burger. Enjoy!

Grilled Brussels Sprouts

Ingredients:

- 1 lb Brussels sprouts, trimmed and halved
- 2-3 tablespoons olive oil

- Salt and pepper, to taste
- Optional seasonings: garlic powder, smoked paprika, lemon zest, Parmesan cheese
- Lemon wedges (for serving, optional)

Instructions:

1. Prepare the Brussels sprouts: Trim the ends of the Brussels sprouts and cut them in half. If they are large, you can quarter them for more even cooking.
2. Marinate or season: In a large bowl, toss the Brussels sprouts with olive oil until evenly coated. Season with salt, pepper, and any optional seasonings you prefer, such as garlic powder, smoked paprika, or lemon zest. Toss well to coat.
3. Preheat the grill: Preheat your grill to medium-high heat. If using wooden skewers, soak them in water for about 15-20 minutes beforehand to prevent burning.
4. Skewer or grill directly: Thread the Brussels sprouts onto skewers or place them directly on the grill grates. If using skewers, leave a bit of space between each sprout to ensure even cooking.
5. Grill the Brussels sprouts: Grill the Brussels sprouts for about 10-15 minutes, turning occasionally with tongs, until they are tender and charred in spots. The cooking time will depend on the size of the Brussels sprouts and the heat of your grill.
6. Serve: Remove the grilled Brussels sprouts from the grill and transfer them to a serving platter. Optionally, squeeze fresh lemon juice over the sprouts before serving for added brightness.

Tips:

- Even cooking: Try to cut the Brussels sprouts into similar sizes to ensure they cook evenly on the grill.
- Variations: Experiment with different seasonings or add-ons like balsamic glaze, honey, or grated Parmesan cheese after grilling for extra flavor.
- Grill basket: If you prefer, you can use a grill basket or grill tray to cook the Brussels sprouts. This can help prevent smaller pieces from falling through the grill grates.

Grilled Brussels sprouts are a delightful side dish that pairs well with grilled meats, seafood, or as part of a vegetarian meal. They're perfect for summer gatherings or any time you want to enjoy a healthy and flavorful dish straight from the grill!

BBQ Tofu Sandwiches

Ingredients:

For the BBQ Tofu:

- 1 block (14-16 oz) extra-firm tofu, drained and pressed
- 1/2 cup BBQ sauce (homemade or store-bought)
- 2 tablespoons soy sauce or tamari
- 2 tablespoons olive oil
- 1 tablespoon maple syrup or brown sugar
- 1 teaspoon smoked paprika
- 1/2 teaspoon garlic powder
- Salt and pepper, to taste

For the Sandwiches:

- Burger buns or sandwich rolls
- Coleslaw (optional, for topping)
- Sliced red onion (optional, for topping)
- Pickles (optional, for topping)

Instructions:

1. Prepare the tofu:
   - Cut the pressed tofu into slices or rectangles, about 1/2 inch thick.
2. Prepare the marinade:
   - In a bowl, whisk together BBQ sauce, soy sauce or tamari, olive oil, maple syrup or brown sugar, smoked paprika, garlic powder, salt, and pepper.
3. Marinate the tofu:
   - Place the tofu slices in a shallow dish or a large zip-top bag. Pour the BBQ marinade over the tofu, making sure each piece is coated evenly. Let it marinate for at least 30 minutes, flipping halfway through to ensure all sides absorb the flavors.
4. Cook the tofu:
   - Heat a grill pan or skillet over medium-high heat. Once hot, add the marinated tofu slices (reserve the marinade for later). Cook for about 3-4 minutes on each side, or until the tofu is golden brown and has grill marks. You can also grill the tofu on an outdoor grill for a smokier flavor.
5. Warm the marinade:
   - While the tofu is cooking, pour the reserved marinade into a small saucepan. Bring to a simmer over medium heat and cook for 5-7 minutes, stirring occasionally, until it thickens slightly. This will be used as a sauce for the sandwiches.
6. Assemble the sandwiches:
   - Toast the burger buns or sandwich rolls lightly, if desired.
   - Place a generous amount of BBQ tofu on the bottom half of each bun.
   - Top with coleslaw, sliced red onion, pickles, or any other toppings you prefer.
   - Drizzle with the warmed BBQ marinade sauce.
7. Serve:

- Close the sandwiches with the top half of the buns and serve immediately while warm.

Tips:

- **Texture:** For a firmer texture, you can bake the marinated tofu in the oven at 400°F (200°C) for about 20-25 minutes instead of grilling.
- **Customization:** Feel free to customize the sandwiches with your favorite toppings and condiments. Avocado slices, fresh greens, or a slice of vegan cheese can also be great additions.
- **Make-ahead:** You can prepare the BBQ tofu ahead of time and store it in the refrigerator until ready to cook. Warm it up before assembling the sandwiches.

BBQ Tofu Sandwiches are a flavorful and nutritious vegetarian option that's sure to be a hit at your next barbecue or meal gathering. Enjoy the smoky, tangy flavors in every bite!

Grilled Carrots

Ingredients:

- 1 lb carrots, peeled and trimmed (you can leave smaller carrots whole, or cut larger ones into halves or quarters lengthwise)
- 2 tablespoons olive oil
- 2 cloves garlic, minced (optional)
- 1 teaspoon ground cumin
- 1 teaspoon smoked paprika
- Salt and pepper, to taste
- Fresh herbs (parsley, thyme, or dill), chopped for garnish (optional)
- Lemon wedges, for serving (optional)

Instructions:

1. Prepare the carrots: If using larger carrots, cut them lengthwise into halves or quarters to ensure even cooking. Leave smaller carrots whole. Ensure they are peeled and trimmed.
2. Prepare the marinade: In a small bowl, whisk together the olive oil, minced garlic (if using), ground cumin, smoked paprika, salt, and pepper.
3. Marinate the carrots: Place the carrots in a shallow dish or large zip-top bag. Pour the marinade over the carrots and toss to coat them evenly. Let them marinate for at least 15-20 minutes, or longer if time allows. This allows the flavors to penetrate the carrots.
4. Preheat the grill: Preheat your grill to medium-high heat.
5. Grill the carrots: Place the marinated carrots directly on the grill grates. Grill for about 8-10 minutes, turning occasionally with tongs, until the carrots are tender and charred in spots. The exact cooking time will depend on the thickness of your carrots and the heat of your grill.
6. Serve: Remove the grilled carrots from the grill and transfer them to a serving platter. Sprinkle with chopped fresh herbs like parsley, thyme, or dill if desired. Serve hot with lemon wedges on the side for an extra burst of freshness.

Tips:

- Grill temperature: Keep an eye on the carrots while grilling to prevent them from burning. Adjust the heat as needed and rotate them occasionally for even cooking.
- Variations: Feel free to customize the marinade with your favorite herbs and spices. You can add a pinch of chili flakes for a spicy kick or a drizzle of balsamic glaze for added sweetness.
- Indoor grilling: If you don't have an outdoor grill, you can also use a grill pan or cook the carrots under the broiler in your oven.

Grilled carrots make a delicious and visually appealing side dish that pairs well with grilled meats, fish, or as part of a vegetarian meal. They're perfect for summer gatherings or any time you want to enjoy fresh, flavorful vegetables straight from the grill!

BBQ Bean Salad

Ingredients:

- 1 can (15 oz) kidney beans, drained and rinsed
- 1 can (15 oz) black beans, drained and rinsed
- 1 can (15 oz) chickpeas (garbanzo beans), drained and rinsed

- 1 red bell pepper, diced
- 1/2 red onion, finely chopped
- 1 cup corn kernels (fresh, canned, or thawed frozen)
- 1/4 cup fresh cilantro or parsley, chopped (optional, for garnish)

For the BBQ Dressing:

- 1/4 cup BBQ sauce (homemade or store-bought)
- 2 tablespoons olive oil
- 1 tablespoon apple cider vinegar or red wine vinegar
- 1 teaspoon Dijon mustard
- 1 clove garlic, minced
- Salt and pepper, to taste

Instructions:

1. Prepare the beans and vegetables: In a large mixing bowl, combine the kidney beans, black beans, chickpeas, diced red bell pepper, chopped red onion, and corn kernels.
2. Make the BBQ dressing: In a small bowl or jar, whisk together the BBQ sauce, olive oil, apple cider vinegar or red wine vinegar, Dijon mustard, minced garlic, salt, and pepper until well combined.
3. Combine and toss: Pour the BBQ dressing over the bean and vegetable mixture. Gently toss until everything is evenly coated with the dressing.
4. Chill and marinate: Cover the bowl and refrigerate the BBQ Bean Salad for at least 30 minutes to allow the flavors to meld together. This step is optional but enhances the taste.
5. Serve: Before serving, give the salad a final toss. Garnish with chopped cilantro or parsley if desired.

Tips:

- Variations: Feel free to customize the salad by adding or substituting other beans such as cannellini beans or pinto beans. You can also add diced tomatoes, avocado chunks, or cucumber for extra freshness.
- Storage: BBQ Bean Salad can be stored in an airtight container in the refrigerator for up to 3-4 days. It's a great make-ahead dish for picnics, barbecues, or meal prep.
- Serve suggestions: Enjoy BBQ Bean Salad as a side dish with grilled meats, fish, or as a standalone vegetarian main dish. It's also delicious served over greens or as a filling for wraps or sandwiches.

BBQ Bean Salad is not only flavorful and satisfying but also packed with protein and fiber from the beans, making it a healthy addition to any meal or gathering.

Grilled Plantains

Ingredients:

- Ripe plantains (1-2 plantains serve 2-4 people, depending on size)
- Olive oil or melted butter (optional)
- Cinnamon (optional, for sprinkling)
- Honey or maple syrup (optional, for drizzling)

Instructions:

1. Prepare the plantains:
   - Choose ripe but firm plantains. Peel the plantains and cut them into diagonal slices, about 1/2 inch thick.
2. Preheat the grill:
   - Preheat your grill to medium-high heat.
3. Brush with oil or butter (optional):
   - Brush both sides of the plantain slices lightly with olive oil or melted butter. This helps prevent sticking and promotes even grilling. Alternatively, you can grill the plantains without oil if you prefer.
4. Grill the plantains:
   - Place the plantain slices directly on the grill grates. Grill for about 2-3 minutes per side, or until grill marks appear and the plantains are tender and slightly caramelized. Use tongs to carefully flip the slices halfway through cooking.
5. Serve:
   - Remove the grilled plantains from the grill and transfer them to a serving platter. Sprinkle with cinnamon if desired and drizzle with honey or maple syrup for added sweetness.

Tips:

- Ripe plantains: Look for plantains that are yellow with some black spots. They should be firm to the touch but not too soft.
- Grill temperature: Monitor the grill temperature to ensure the plantains cook evenly without burning. Adjust the heat as needed.
- Variations: You can experiment with different seasonings such as nutmeg, cardamom, or a sprinkle of sea salt for a savory twist.

Grilled plantains make a delicious side dish or dessert on their own, or they can be served alongside grilled meats or seafood for a sweet and savory contrast. Enjoy the natural sweetness and caramelized flavor of grilled plantains straight from the grill!

BBQ Falafel

Ingredients:

For the BBQ Falafel:

- 1 can (15 oz) chickpeas, drained and rinsed
- 1/2 cup chopped fresh parsley
- 1/2 cup chopped fresh cilantro

- 3 cloves garlic, minced
- 1 small onion, chopped
- 2 tablespoons BBQ sauce (homemade or store-bought)
- 1 tablespoon olive oil
- 1 teaspoon ground cumin
- 1 teaspoon ground coriander
- 1/2 teaspoon smoked paprika
- Salt and pepper, to taste
- 1/4 cup chickpea flour or all-purpose flour (for binding, optional)

For Serving:

- Pita bread or flatbreads
- Tzatziki sauce or tahini sauce
- Sliced tomatoes
- Shredded lettuce or cabbage
- Sliced cucumber
- Pickles or pickled vegetables

Instructions:

1. Prepare the BBQ Falafel mixture:
   - In a food processor, combine the chickpeas, chopped parsley, chopped cilantro, minced garlic, chopped onion, BBQ sauce, olive oil, ground cumin, ground coriander, smoked paprika, salt, and pepper. Pulse until the mixture is well combined and forms a coarse paste. If the mixture is too wet, add chickpea flour or all-purpose flour as needed to bind the ingredients together.
2. Form the falafel patties:
   - Using your hands, shape the falafel mixture into small patties or balls, about 1-2 inches in diameter. Place them on a plate or baking sheet lined with parchment paper.
3. Preheat the grill:
   - Preheat your grill to medium-high heat. Brush the grill grates lightly with oil to prevent sticking.
4. Grill the falafel:
   - Carefully place the falafel patties on the preheated grill. Grill for about 3-4 minutes on each side, or until golden brown and crispy. Use a spatula to gently flip them halfway through cooking.
5. Warm the pita bread or flatbreads:
   - While the falafel is grilling, warm the pita bread or flatbreads on the grill for a minute or two on each side until they are lightly toasted and warm.
6. Assemble the BBQ Falafel sandwiches:
   - Spread a dollop of tzatziki sauce or tahini sauce on each warmed pita bread or flatbread.
   - Place a few grilled BBQ falafel patties on top.

- Add sliced tomatoes, shredded lettuce or cabbage, sliced cucumber, and pickles or pickled vegetables.
7. Serve:
    - Fold or roll up the pita bread or flatbread around the filling to form a sandwich. Serve immediately while warm.

Tips:

- Grill temperature: Keep an eye on the falafel patties while grilling to prevent burning. Adjust the heat as needed.
- Variations: You can customize your BBQ falafel sandwiches with additional toppings such as hummus, chopped onions, roasted red peppers, or a sprinkle of sumac for extra flavor.
- Make-ahead: Prepare the falafel mixture ahead of time and store it in the refrigerator until ready to grill. This allows the flavors to meld together.

BBQ Falafel sandwiches are a delicious and satisfying vegetarian option that's perfect for a barbecue or casual meal. Enjoy the smoky flavors and crunchy texture of grilled falafel combined with fresh vegetables and creamy sauces!

Grilled Pineapple Salsa

Ingredients:

- 1 small pineapple, peeled, cored, and sliced into rings or wedges
- 1 red bell pepper, diced
- 1/2 red onion, finely chopped
- 1 jalapeño pepper, seeded and finely chopped (optional, for heat)
- 1/4 cup fresh cilantro, chopped
- Juice of 1 lime

- Salt and pepper, to taste

Instructions:

1. Preheat the grill:
   - Preheat your grill to medium-high heat.
2. Grill the pineapple:
   - Lightly oil the grill grates to prevent sticking. Place the pineapple slices or wedges directly on the grill. Grill for about 3-4 minutes on each side, or until grill marks appear and the pineapple is caramelized and slightly softened. Remove from the grill and let cool slightly.
3. Prepare the salsa:
   - Once the grilled pineapple has cooled, chop it into small pieces. In a medium bowl, combine the chopped grilled pineapple, diced red bell pepper, finely chopped red onion, chopped jalapeño pepper (if using), and chopped cilantro.
4. Season the salsa:
   - Add fresh lime juice, salt, and pepper to taste. Gently toss all the ingredients together until well combined.
5. Chill and serve:
   - Refrigerate the grilled pineapple salsa for at least 30 minutes to allow the flavors to meld together before serving. This step is optional but enhances the taste.
6. Serve:
   - Serve the grilled pineapple salsa chilled or at room temperature. It pairs wonderfully with grilled meats such as chicken or pork, fish tacos, or as a topping for quesadillas or nachos.

Tips:

- Grill variations: If you prefer, you can also grill the red bell pepper and red onion alongside the pineapple for added smoky flavor.
- Customization: Adjust the heat level of the salsa by adding more or less jalapeño pepper, or leave it out entirely for a mild version.
- Storage: Grilled pineapple salsa can be stored in an airtight container in the refrigerator for up to 3 days. Stir well before serving leftovers.

Grilled pineapple salsa is a vibrant and delicious addition to any summer meal or barbecue. Enjoy the combination of sweet, smoky, and tangy flavors in every bite!

BBQ Spaghetti Squash

Ingredients:

- 1 medium spaghetti squash
- Olive oil
- Salt and pepper, to taste
- BBQ sauce (homemade or store-bought)
- Optional toppings: chopped fresh herbs (parsley or cilantro), grated cheese (Parmesan or cheddar), diced red onion

Instructions:

1. Prepare the spaghetti squash:
   - Preheat your oven to 400°F (200°C).
   - Carefully cut the spaghetti squash in half lengthwise. Scoop out the seeds and stringy pulp with a spoon.
   - Brush the cut sides of the squash with olive oil and sprinkle with salt and pepper.
2. Roast the spaghetti squash:
   - Place the squash halves, cut side down, on a baking sheet lined with parchment paper or foil.
   - Roast in the preheated oven for 40-50 minutes, or until the squash is tender and easily pierced with a fork.
3. Prepare the BBQ sauce:
   - While the squash is roasting, prepare your favorite BBQ sauce if using homemade. Otherwise, have your store-bought BBQ sauce ready.
4. Shred the squash:
   - Once the spaghetti squash is cooked and cool enough to handle, use a fork to scrape the flesh into strands. Transfer the strands to a mixing bowl.
5. Combine with BBQ sauce:
   - Add your desired amount of BBQ sauce to the shredded spaghetti squash. Start with a few tablespoons and adjust to your taste preferences. Toss well to coat the squash evenly with the sauce.
6. Serve:
   - Transfer the BBQ spaghetti squash mixture to serving plates or bowls. Optionally, top with chopped fresh herbs, grated cheese, and diced red onion for added flavor and texture.

Tips:

- Grilling option: Instead of roasting, you can also grill the spaghetti squash. Cut it in half, brush with olive oil and season with salt and pepper. Grill cut-side down over medium heat for about 20-30 minutes until tender. Then scrape out the flesh and proceed with mixing in BBQ sauce.
- Customization: Feel free to customize your BBQ spaghetti squash with additional toppings such as cooked shredded chicken, black beans, avocado slices, or sour cream.
- Storage: Store any leftover BBQ spaghetti squash in an airtight container in the refrigerator for up to 3-4 days. Reheat gently in the microwave or on the stovetop.

BBQ spaghetti squash is a healthy and satisfying dish that's perfect as a vegetarian main course or a flavorful side dish. Enjoy the smoky sweetness of BBQ sauce combined with the natural texture of spaghetti squash for a delicious meal!

Grilled Mango

Ingredients:

- 2 ripe mangoes
- Olive oil or melted butter, for brushing (optional)
- Honey or maple syrup, for drizzling (optional)
- Fresh lime juice, for squeezing (optional)
- Mint leaves or cilantro, chopped for garnish (optional)
- Vanilla ice cream or Greek yogurt, for serving (optional)

Instructions:

1. Prepare the mangoes:
   - Choose ripe but firm mangoes. Peel the mangoes and cut them into thick slices or wedges, about 1/2 to 3/4 inch thick.
2. Preheat the grill:
   - Preheat your grill to medium-high heat.
3. Brush with oil or butter (optional):
   - Brush both sides of the mango slices lightly with olive oil or melted butter. This helps prevent sticking and promotes even grilling. Alternatively, you can grill the mango slices without oil if you prefer.
4. Grill the mango:
   - Place the mango slices directly on the grill grates. Grill for about 2-3 minutes on each side, or until grill marks appear and the mango is caramelized and slightly softened. Use tongs to carefully flip the slices halfway through cooking.
5. Serve:
   - Remove the grilled mango slices from the grill and transfer them to a serving platter. Drizzle with honey or maple syrup, squeeze fresh lime juice over them if desired, and sprinkle with chopped mint leaves or cilantro for added freshness.
6. Optional serving ideas:
   - Serve grilled mango slices on their own as a light and refreshing dessert.
   - Pair them with vanilla ice cream or Greek yogurt for a creamy contrast.
   - Add grilled mango slices to salads, salsa, or as a topping for grilled meats or seafood.

Tips:

- Grill temperature: Monitor the grill temperature to ensure the mango slices cook evenly without burning. Adjust the heat as needed.
- Variations: You can sprinkle the grilled mango slices with a pinch of chili powder or ground cinnamon for a spicy or warm flavor profile.
- Storage: Grilled mango slices are best enjoyed fresh off the grill. If you have leftovers, store them in an airtight container in the refrigerator for up to 2 days.

Grilled mango is a delicious and versatile dish that's perfect for summer gatherings, BBQs, or as a simple and elegant dessert. Enjoy the sweet, caramelized flavors straight from the grill!

BBQ Beyond Burgers

Ingredients:

- Beyond Burger patties (as many as needed)
- BBQ sauce (homemade or store-bought)
- Burger buns
- Optional toppings: lettuce, tomato slices, red onion slices, pickles, vegan cheese slices

Instructions:

1. Preheat the grill:
   - Preheat your grill to medium-high heat.
2. Grill the Beyond Burger patties:
   - Place the Beyond Burger patties directly on the grill grates. Grill for about 3-4 minutes on each side, or until they are heated through and grill marks appear. The cooking time may vary depending on the thickness of the patties and the heat of your grill.
3. Brush with BBQ sauce:
   - Brush each side of the Beyond Burger patties with BBQ sauce during the last minute or two of grilling. This allows the sauce to caramelize and infuse flavor into the patties.
4. Toast the burger buns:
   - While the patties are grilling, you can also toast the burger buns on the grill until they are lightly golden and warm.
5. Assemble the BBQ Beyond Burgers:
   - Place each grilled Beyond Burger patty on a toasted bun.
   - Add your desired toppings such as lettuce, tomato slices, red onion slices, pickles, and vegan cheese slices.
6. Serve:
   - Serve the BBQ Beyond Burgers immediately while warm, alongside your favorite side dishes or salads.

Tips:

- Grilling Beyond Burgers: Beyond Burger patties cook relatively quickly on the grill. Avoid overcooking to maintain their juiciness and texture.
- Customization: Feel free to customize your BBQ Beyond Burgers with different types of BBQ sauce or additional toppings according to your preferences.
- Accompaniments: Serve BBQ Beyond Burgers with classic sides like potato salad, coleslaw, or sweet potato fries for a complete meal.

BBQ Beyond Burgers are a flavorful and protein-packed option for those looking to enjoy a plant-based meal with the smoky goodness of BBQ flavors. They're perfect for summer cookouts or any time you crave a delicious veggie burger straight from the grill!

Grilled Polenta

Ingredients:

- 1 cup polenta (coarse cornmeal)
- 4 cups water or vegetable broth
- Salt, to taste
- Olive oil, for brushing
- Optional toppings: grated Parmesan cheese, chopped fresh herbs (such as parsley or basil), marinara sauce

Instructions:

1. Cook the polenta:

    - In a medium saucepan, bring 4 cups of water or vegetable broth to a boil. Gradually whisk in the polenta and reduce the heat to low. Stir continuously to prevent lumps from forming.
2. Simmer the polenta:
    - Cook the polenta over low heat, stirring frequently, until it thickens and becomes creamy. This usually takes about 20-30 minutes. Add salt to taste.
3. Prepare the polenta for grilling:
    - Pour the cooked polenta into a lightly greased baking dish or rimmed baking sheet lined with parchment paper. Smooth it out evenly with a spatula. Allow it to cool and set for at least 30 minutes.
4. Preheat the grill:
    - Preheat your grill to medium-high heat. Brush the grill grates lightly with olive oil to prevent sticking.
5. Grill the polenta:
    - Once the polenta has set, use a sharp knife to cut it into squares or rectangles, about 1/2 to 3/4 inch thick.
    - Carefully transfer the polenta pieces to the preheated grill. Grill for about 4-5 minutes on each side, or until grill marks appear and the polenta is crispy and lightly browned.
6. Serve:
    - Remove the grilled polenta from the grill and arrange it on a serving platter. Serve hot, optionally topped with grated Parmesan cheese, chopped fresh herbs, or marinara sauce.

Tips:

- Polenta consistency: For grilling, it's important that the polenta sets and firms up after cooking. This helps it hold together better on the grill.
- Grilling time: Cooking times may vary depending on the thickness of your polenta slices and the heat of your grill. Keep an eye on them to prevent burning.
- Variations: Experiment with different seasonings or additions to the polenta before grilling, such as garlic powder, dried herbs, or a sprinkle of paprika for added flavor.

Grilled polenta is a versatile dish that pairs well with a variety of toppings and accompaniments. Enjoy its crispy exterior and creamy interior as a side dish or a base for other grilled vegetables or meats!

www.ingramcontent.com/pod-product-compliance
Lightning Source LLC
LaVergne TN
LVHW062047070526

838201LV00080B/2159